BAPTISTWAY ADULT BIBLE STUDY GUIDE®

The Gospel of Matthew
A PRIMER FOR DISCIPLESHIP

JULIE BROWN WOOD
PHIL LINEBERGER
BOB DEFOOR
RONNY MARRIOTT

BAPTISTWAYPRESS®
Dallas, Texas

The Gospel of Matthew: A Primer for Discipleship—BaptistWay Adult Bible Study Guide®

BAPTISTWAY PRESS® Leadership Team
Associate Executive Director, Baptist General Convention of Texas: Steve Vernon
Director, Education/Discipleship Center: Chris Liebrum
Director, Bible Study/Discipleship Team: Phil Miller
Publisher, BAPTISTWAY PRESS®: Ross West

Cover and Interior Design and Production: Desktop Miracles, Inc.
Printing: Data Reproductions Corporation

First edition: December 2011
ISBN–13: 978-1-934731-80-2

How to Make the Best Use of This Issue

Whether you're the teacher or a student—

1. Start early in the week before your class meets.

2. Overview the study. Review the table of contents and read the study introduction. Try to see how each lesson relates to the overall study.

3. Use your Bible to read and consider prayerfully the Scripture passages for the lesson. (You'll see that each writer has chosen a favorite translation for the lessons in this issue. You're free to use the Bible translation you prefer and compare it with the translation chosen for that unit, of course.)

4. After reading all the Scripture passages in your Bible, then read the writer's comments. The comments are intended to be an aid to your study of the Bible.

5. Read the small articles—"sidebars"—in each lesson. They are intended to provide additional, enrichment information and inspiration and to encourage thought and application.

6. Try to answer for yourself the questions included in each lesson. They're intended to encourage further thought and application, and they can also be used in the class session itself.

If you're the teacher—

A. Do all of the things just mentioned, of course. As you begin the study with your class, be sure to find a way to help your class know the date on which each lesson will be studied. You might do this in one or more of the following ways:

    • In the first session of the study, briefly overview the study by identifying with your class the date on which each lesson will be studied. Lead your class to write the date in the table of contents on page 9 and on the first page of each lesson.

- Make and post a chart that indicates the date on which each lesson will be studied.

- If all of your class has e-mail, send them an e-mail with the dates the lessons will be studied.

- Provide a bookmark with the lesson dates. You may want to include information about your church and then use the bookmark as an outreach tool, too. A model for a bookmark can be downloaded from www.baptistwaypress.org on the Resources for Adults page.

- Develop a sticker with the lesson dates, and place it on the table of contents or on the back cover.

B. Get a copy of the *Teaching Guide*, a companion piece to this *Study Guide*. The *Teaching Guide* contains additional Bible comments plus two teaching plans. The teaching plans in the *Teaching Guide* are intended to provide practical, easy-to-use teaching suggestions that will work in your class.

C. After you've studied the Bible passage, the lesson comments, and other material, use the teaching suggestions in the *Teaching Guide* to help you develop your plan for leading your class in studying each lesson.

D. Teaching resource items for use as handouts are available free at www.baptistwaypress.org.

E. You may want to get the additional adult Bible study comments— *Adult Online Bible Commentary*—by Dr. Jim Denison (president, Denison Forum on Truth and Culture, and theologian-in-residence, Baptist General Convention of Texas). Call 1–866–249–1799 or e-mail baptistway@texasbaptists.org to order *Adult Online Bible Commentary*. It is available only in electronic format (PDF) from our website. The price of these comments is $6 for individuals and $25 for a group of five. A church or class that participates in our advance order program for free shipping can receive *Adult Online Bible Commentary* free. Call 1–866–249–1799 or see www.baptistwaypress.org to purchase or for information on participating in our free shipping program for the next study.

F. Additional teaching plans are also available in electronic format (PDF) by calling 1–866–249–1799. The price of these additional teaching plans is $5 for an individual and $20 for a group of five. A church or class that participates in our advance order program for free shipping can receive *Adult Online Teaching Plans* free. Call 1–866–249–1799 or see www.baptistwaypress.org for information on participating in our free shipping program for the next study.

G. You also may want to get the enrichment teaching help that is provided on the internet by the *Baptist Standard* at www.baptiststandard.com. (Other class participants may find this information helpful, too.) Call 214–630–4571 to begin your subscription to the printed or electronic edition of the *Baptist Standard*.

H. Enjoy leading your class in discovering the meaning of the Scripture passages and in applying these passages to their lives.

Note: The time of the first release of these materials includes the Christmas holiday. To meet the needs of churches who wish to have a Bible study lesson specifically on the Christmas Scripture passages at this time, a Christmas lesson is included.

DO YOU USE A KINDLE?

This BaptistWay *Adult Bible Study Guide* plus *Profiles in Character; The Gospel of John: Part One; The Gospel of John: Part Two;* and *The Corinthian Letters: Imperatives for an Imperfect Church* are now available in a Kindle edition. The easiest way to find these materials is to search for "BaptistWay" on your Kindle or go to www.amazon.com/kindle and do a search for "BaptistWay." The Kindle edition can be studied not only on a Kindle but also on a PC, Mac, iPhone, Blackberry, or Android phone using the Kindle app available free from amazon.com/kindle.

Audio Bible Study Lessons

Do you want to use your walk/run/ride, etc. time to study the Bible? Or maybe you're a college student who wants to listen to the lesson on your iPod®? Or maybe you're looking for a way to study the Bible when you just can't find time to read? Or maybe you know someone who has difficulty seeing to read even our *Large Print Study Guide*?

Then try our audio Bible study lessons, available on this study plus *Profiles in Character; The Gospel of Luke; The Gospel of John: Part One; The Gospel of John: Part Two; The Corinthian Letters: Imperatives for an Imperfect Church; Galatians and 1 & 2 Thessalonians;* and *The Letters of James and John.* For more information or to order, call 1–866–249–1799 or e-mail baptistway@texasbaptists.org. The files are downloaded from our website. You'll need an audio player that plays MP3 files (like an iPod®, but many MP3 players are available), or you can listen on a computer.

Writers of This Study Guide

Julie (Brown) Wood, writer of lessons one through three, is a graduate of Hardin-Simmons University and Southwestern Baptist Theological Seminary. She loves ministering with her husband, Dr. Darin Wood, pastor of Central Baptist Church in Jacksonville, Texas, and being mother to their son, Joshua. A former children's minister and worship leader, she now serves as a freelance writer and as pianist for Jacksonville Independent School District choirs.

Phil Lineberger, writer of lessons four through eight, is pastor of Sugar Land Baptist Church, Sugar Land, Texas (formerly known as Williams Trace Baptist Church). Phil is married to Brenda, with three daughters and nine grandchildren. He has served as president of the Baptist General Convention of Texas, as a trustee for William Jewell College and Dallas Baptist University, as a regent at Baylor University, and as vice-president of the Cotton Bowl Athletic Association.

Bob DeFoor of Harrodsburg, Kentucky, wrote lessons nine, ten, and the Christmas lesson. Dr. DeFoor served more than forty years as a pastor of churches in Kentucky and Georgia, serving the last twenty-eight prior to retirement as pastor of Harrodsburg Baptist Church. Both Bob and his wife Sandy are native Georgians, and both are graduates of Baylor University.

Ronny Marriott wrote lessons eleven through thirteen and also "Teaching Plans" in the *Adult Bible Teaching Guide* for these lessons. Dr. Marriott is pastor of First Baptist Church, Corpus Christi, Texas. He holds the Doctor of Ministry degree from Southwestern Baptist Theological Seminary.

The Gospel of Matthew: A Primer for Discipleship

Introducing

THE GOSPEL OF MATTHEW:
A Primer for Discipleship

A Primer for Discipleship?

A "primer" is an elementary textbook. While the Gospel of Matthew may not seem elementary, the early church recognized its usefulness as a basic instruction book on what being a follower of Jesus means. A major purpose of the Gospel of Matthew is instruction for discipleship.

Can there be any doubt that today's church needs a book like this and needs to give attention—elementary attention, even—to discipleship? The word "Christian" is bandied about so loosely and applied to so many entities and actions, with some of them having a questionable connection with Jesus if any at all. Too, many people call themselves "Christians," with little apparent attention to what the word means.

So don't we need to return to the New Testament to discover what exactly being "Christian" means? Being Christian is not about merely *getting saved*. *Salvation* is indeed important, but it is often talked about in a misguided, superficial manner. Being Christian is about being a disciple of Jesus. When we are disciples of Jesus, we can trust Jesus to take care of our salvation.

The Priority of Discipleship

Dietrich Bonhoeffer, the German Christian who was martyred by Hitler in the closing days of World War II, wrote in his classic book *The Cost of Discipleship* that Christianity is not about adhering to an abstract idea or set of teachings but rather is about adhering to Christ, following Christ, being a disciple of Christ. As Bonhoeffer wrote so eloquently, "Christianity without the living Christ is inevitably Christianity without discipleship, and Christianity without discipleship is always Christianity without Christ."[1] Bonhoeffer spoke of "cheap grace," which he defined as "grace without discipleship."[2] Bonhoeffer's *The Cost of Discipleship* relies on the Gospel of Matthew as a guide to genuine discipleship.

Baptist author Dallas Willard in his book *The Divine Conspiracy* also makes frequent reference to the Gospel of Matthew. In *The Divine Conspiracy*, Willard writes of "A Curriculum for Christlikeness," definitely a needed curriculum.[3] In speaking of the need for such a curriculum on discipleship, he uses the image of learning to ride a bicycle. He states, "When you teach children or adults to ride a bicycle or swim, they actually do ride bikes and swim. . . . You don't just teach them that they *ought* to ride bicycles, or that it is *good* to ride bicycles, or that they should be ashamed if they don't."[4]

Yet that is what happens in too many churches and Bible study classes with the instructions on discipleship in the Scriptures, including the Gospel of Matthew. That is not what we want to happen in this study.

This study of the Gospel of Matthew is indeed a study of the Gospel of Matthew. It moves sequentially through the Gospel. The Scriptures selected for study, though, relate specifically to the matter of discipleship. The study is intended to focus on discipleship as a major theme in the Gospel of Matthew. The study will encourage seeing that the Gospel of Matthew indeed is "a primer for discipleship."

Further, to be as clear as possible, the intent is not that you learn from this study that you *ought* to live as Jesus' disciple, or that it would be *good* if you were to live as Jesus' disciple, or that you should be *ashamed* if you don't live as Jesus' disciple. Rather, the intent of this study is that you learn to *actually live* as Jesus' disciple. An additional intent is that you participate with your church in focusing on *actually doing what Jesus commanded* us to do: "make disciples . . . baptizing them in the name of the Father and of the Son and of the Holy Spirit, and teaching them to obey everything I have commanded you" (Matthew 28:19–20).

How the Study Is Developed

Unit one, "Learning Who Jesus Is," contains three lessons from Matthew 1—4. The first two lessons attempt to focus on Matthew's purpose in the events of Jesus' birth and baptism, to show Jesus' identity and emphasize that Jesus is worthy to be followed. Lesson three deals with Jesus' call of the first disciples.

Unit two, "Learning from Jesus," consists of five lessons that emphasize instructions for disciples. These lessons study Jesus' "Discourse on Discipleship" in Matthew 5—7, known as the Sermon on the Mount.[5]

Unit three, "Further Instructions on Genuine Discipleship," provides further instructions that clarify the nature of discipleship. The four lessons in this unit deal with passages selected from Matthew 8—16 that speak pointedly to the nature of being Jesus' disciple.

Unit four, "Following Jesus' Command," consists of one lesson on Jesus' command, "Make disciples," in Matthew 28:16–20.

Note: The time of the first release of these materials includes the Christmas season. To meet the needs of churches and classes who wish to have a Bible study lesson specifically on the Christmas Scripture passages at this time, a Christmas lesson is included.

UNIT ONE. LEARNING WHO JESUS IS		
Lesson 1	The Birth of Jesus the Messiah	Matthew 1:18—2:15, 19–23
Lesson 2	God's Beloved Son, Baptized by John	Matthew 3
Lesson 3	Called to Follow Jesus	Matthew 4:12–22
UNIT TWO. LEARNING FROM JESUS		
Lesson 4	The Distinctive Life of Disciples	Matthew 5:1–16
Lesson 5	Live By Jesus' Interpretation of God's Will	Matthew 5:17–48
Lesson 6	Show Your Faith This Way—Not That Way	Matthew 6:1–18
Lesson 7	Trust God and Stop Worrying About Things	Matthew 6:19–34
Lesson 8	Make the Right Choice	Matthew 7:1–27

Additional Resources for Studying the Gospel of Matthew: A Primer for Discipleship[6]

Craig L. Blomberg. *Matthew*. The New American Commentary. Nashville: Broadman Press, 1992.

Dietrich Bonhoeffer. *The Cost of Discipleship*. New York: Simon & Schuster, Touchstone Book, 1995 (originally published in German in 1937).

M. Eugene Boring. "Matthew." *The New Interpreter's Bible*. Volume VIII. Nashville: Abingdon Press, 1995.

R.T. France. *The Gospel of Matthew*. The New International Commentary on the New Testament. Grand Rapids, Michigan: William B. Eerdmans Publishing Company, 2007.

David Garland. *Reading Matthew*. Macon, Georgia: Smyth and Helwys Publishing, Inc., 1999.

Craig S. Keener. *IVP Bible Background Commentary: New Testament*. Downers Grove, Illinois: InterVarsity Press, 1994.

Craig S. Keener. *The Gospel of Matthew*. IVP New Testament Commentary. Downers Grove, Illinois: InterVarsity Press, 1997.

Douglas R. A. Hare. *Matthew*. Interpretation: A Bible Commentary for Teaching and Preaching. Louisville: John Knox Press, 1993.

A.T. Robertson. "The Gospel of Matthew." *Word Pictures in the New Testament*. Volume 1. Nashville, Tennessee: Broadman Press, 1930.

Frank Stagg. "Matthew." *The Broadman Bible Commentary*. Volume 8. Nashville: Broadman Press, 1969.

Dallas Willard. *The Divine Conspiracy: Rediscovering Our Hidden Life in God*. San Francisco: HarperSanFrancisco, 1998.

NOTES

1. Dietrich Bonhoeffer, *The Cost of Discipleship* (New York: Simon & Schuster, Touchstone Book, 1995), 63–64.

2. Bonhoeffer, *The Cost of Discipleship*, 47.

3. Dallas Willard, *The Divine Conspiracy: Rediscovering Our Hidden Life in God* (San Francisco: HarperSanFrancisco, 1998), 311.

4. Willard, 314, italics in the original.

5. R.T. France, *The Gospel of Matthew*, The New International Commentary on the New Testament (Grand Rapids, Michigan: William B. Eerdmans Publishing Company, 2007), see on Matthew 5:1—7:29 introduction.

6. Listing a book does not imply full agreement by the writers or BAPTISTWAY PRESS® with all of its comments.

—————————— U N I T   O N E ——————————

Learning Who Jesus Is

Unit one, "Learning Who Jesus Is," contains three lessons from Matthew 1—4. The first two lessons attempt to focus on Matthew's purpose in telling the events of Jesus' birth and baptism. Seen from the perspective of Matthew's theme of providing instruction for disciples, these events show Jesus' identity and emphasize that Jesus is worthy to be followed. Lesson three deals with Jesus' call of the first disciples.

FOCAL TEXT
Matthew 1:18–2:15, 19–23

BACKGROUND
Matthew 1—2

MAIN IDEA
The circumstances of
Jesus' birth show that he
is the Messiah and thus
worthy to be followed.

QUESTION TO EXPLORE
How do the circumstances of
Jesus' birth show him worth
following as his disciple?

STUDY AIM
To identify from the
circumstances of Jesus'
birth why Jesus is worth
following as his disciple

QUICK READ
Jesus' miraculous beginnings
fulfilled prophecy, proving
him to be the Promised
One who is fully God and
fully human for all people
to worship and follow.

LESSON ONE
The Birth of Jesus the Messiah

Matthew revealed God's heart for people of all nations. He wrote so that those who follow Christ might know who Jesus is in order to be informed and effective disciples. Matthew's Gospel begins with the birth and birthright of Jesus (Matthew 1) and continues to the recording of the Great Commission (Matt. 28:19–20). One reason Jesus is worthy to be worshiped and followed is his miraculous beginning.

MATTHEW 1:18–25

[18] This is how the birth of Jesus Christ came about: His mother Mary was pledged to be married to Joseph, but before they came together, she was found to be with child through the Holy Spirit. [19] Because Joseph her husband was a righteous man and did not want to expose her to public disgrace, he had in mind to divorce her quietly.

[20] But after he had considered this, an angel of the Lord appeared to him in a dream and said, "Joseph son of David, do not be afraid to take Mary home as your wife, because what is conceived in her is from the Holy Spirit. [21] She will give birth to a son, and you are to give him the name Jesus, because he will save his people from their sins."

[22] All this took place to fulfill what the Lord had said through the prophet: [23] "The virgin will be with child and will give birth to a son, and they will call him Immanuel"—which means, "God with us."

[24] When Joseph woke up, he did what the angel of the Lord had commanded him and took Mary home as his wife. [25] But he had no union with her until she gave birth to a son. And he gave him the name Jesus.

MATTHEW 2:1–15, 19–23

[1] After Jesus was born in Bethlehem in Judea, during the time of King Herod, Magi from the east came to Jerusalem [2] and asked, "Where is the one who has been born king of the Jews? We saw his star in the east and have come to worship him."

³ When King Herod heard this he was disturbed, and all Jerusalem with him. ⁴ When he had called together all the people's chief priests and teachers of the law, he asked them where the Christ was to be born. ⁵ "In Bethlehem in Judea," they replied, "for this is what the prophet has written:
⁶ "'But you, Bethlehem, in the land of Judah,
   are by no means least among the rulers of Judah;
for out of you will come a ruler
   who will be the shepherd of my people Israel.'"
⁷ Then Herod called the Magi secretly and found out from them the exact time the star had appeared. ⁸ He sent them to Bethlehem and said, "Go and make a careful search for the child. As soon as you find him, report to me, so that I too may go and worship him."
⁹ After they had heard the king, they went on their way, and the star they had seen in the east went ahead of them until it stopped over the place where the child was. ¹⁰ When they saw the star, they were overjoyed. ¹¹ On coming to the house, they saw the child with his mother Mary, and they bowed down and worshiped him. Then they opened their treasures and presented him with gifts of gold and of incense and of myrrh. ¹² And having been warned in a dream not to go back to Herod, they returned to their country by another route.
¹³ When they had gone, an angel of the Lord appeared to Joseph in a dream. "Get up," he said, "take the child and his mother and escape to Egypt. Stay there until I tell you, for Herod is going to search for the child to kill him."
¹⁴ So he got up, took the child and his mother during the night and left for Egypt, ¹⁵ where he stayed until the death of Herod. And so was fulfilled what the Lord had said through the prophet: "Out of Egypt I called my son."

·   ·   ·   ·   ·   ·   ·   ·   ·   ·   ·   ·   ·   ·   ·   ·   ·   ·   ·

¹⁹ After Herod died, an angel of the Lord appeared in a dream to Joseph in Egypt ²⁰ and said, "Get up, take the child and his mother and go to the land of Israel, for those who were trying to take the child's life are dead."

> ²¹ So he got up, took the child and his mother and went to the land of Israel. ²² But when he heard that Archelaus was reigning in Judea in place of his father Herod, he was afraid to go there. Having been warned in a dream, he withdrew to the district of Galilee, ²³ and he went and lived in a town called Nazareth. So was fulfilled what was said through the prophets: "He will be called a Nazarene."

Surprise! (1:18–25)

Matthew used the first part of chapter 1 to establish the humanity of Jesus and the last part to affirm his divinity. Verses 1–17 reveal Jesus as a son of David and Abraham, as Scripture prophesied of the Messiah. Matthew's first-century Jewish Christian audience was male-oriented, thus suggesting why Matthew's narrative is seen through the experiences of Joseph. The citations of Old Testament passages to affirm Christ's divinity through fulfillment of prophecies would also have appealed to readers' Jewish heritage.

Mary and Joseph's betrothal (1:18) was a formal pre-nuptial contract arranged by parents and entered into before witnesses. It was legally binding, requiring a divorce to break it, although living together and sexual relations were not permitted during this time. If one partner died during the betrothal period, the other was considered widowed. Usually about a year following the signing of the contract, a formal public marriage ceremony took place. To contrast Jesus' conception with pagan legends that crassly told of gods having sexual relations with women, Matthew distinguished Mary's pregnancy as "through the Holy Spirit." Jesus' conception was both supernatural and natural and revealed Jesus as both Son of God and Son of Man.

Joseph was certainly not sinless, but he had integrity and sought to obey God's instructions (1:19). Jewish law entitled him to expose Mary as an adulteress through a public trial; instead, he planned to spare her disgrace and a death sentence (Leviticus 20:10). Nevertheless, as a righteous man, Joseph would not marry a woman he believed unfaithful.

Therefore, his plan was a quiet divorce. This out-of-court settlement would take place before only two witnesses as he gave her a writ of divorcement and paid a fine. However, an angel appeared to Joseph in a dream, assuring Joseph of Mary's fidelity and instructing him to follow through with the marriage because the child she bore was "from the Holy Spirit" (Matt. 1:20–21). The angel's declaration of the child's name, "Jesus" (Hebrew *Yeshua/Joshua*), meaning *the Lord saves*, fulfilled a divine promise of deliverance, for this child would save "his people," from their sins. This act would provide spiritual reconciliation with God for sinful humanity (see 26:28).

Biblical prophecy can be viewed through several lenses. A single prophecy may explain the past, interpret the present, and/or predict the future. In verses 22–23, Matthew cited Isaiah 7:14, introducing the first of many Old Testament fulfillment quotations. Isaiah's understanding of his prophecy was probably a promise to King Ahaz of a *virgin* or *maiden* (Hebrew *almah*) giving birth to a son (perhaps Hezekiah). Thus, this prophecy was partially fulfilled in Isaiah's time but completely fulfilled by Jesus. Matthew's translation of the Hebrew "Immanuel" (Matt. 1:23) confirmed Jesus' saving task was to be God's presence with humanity.

Joseph obeyed God by marrying Mary and naming the child Jesus (1:24). By participating in Jesus' naming, Joseph was viewed as the legal father, thereby securing Jesus' place through his Davidic lineage. Nevertheless, to deny claims of Joseph's biological paternity, Matthew restated Christ's miraculous conception, indicating Joseph and Mary's abstinence from sexual intercourse until after she gave birth (1:25).

Which Way to the Baby? (2:1–11)

How much time elapsed between Jesus' birth and the visit of the Magi is not stated. Matthew mentioned the family was in a "house" (2:11), and so Jesus was in more permanent housing and no longer lying in a manger. Tradition holds these visitors arrived twelve days later, a day celebrated by many believers as Epiphany, January 6 (see small article, "Christmas Day Is Here—or There"). Others believe one to two years elapsed between the time the Magi saw the star until they arrived to worship him.

Herod the Great, king of the Judean region 37–4 B.C., is recorded in history as a shrewd diplomat and an excellent administrator, providing superb famine relief and great public works projects. Part Edomite and part Hebrew, he claimed himself a subscriber to Judaism and expressed sympathies with Israelites under Roman control. He attempted to prove his relation to Judaism by rebuilding the temple, meanwhile demanding oppressive taxes. Love for power, however, became an obsession. Fearing threats to his throne and plots to overthrow him, he had family members put to death. Caesar Augustus punned he would rather be Herod's pig (Greek *hys*) than his son (Greek *huios*).

Obviously, with this kind of paranoia, Herod was troubled (2:3) when he learned visiting Magi were in Jerusalem asking, "Where is the one who has been born king of the Jews?" The Greek word for Herod's and Jerusalem's responses figuratively describes someone in acute emotional distress or turmoil. Herod was deeply disturbed, and all Jerusalem feared his response, or even Roman retaliation against a Jewish rival. The Magi's question was significant in two respects: (1) "born" states a legitimate blood claim to royalty while Herod was merely appointed; and (2) "is" implied that Jesus was already king of the Jews.[1] Herod sensed a threat, and it didn't help that the Magi desired to "worship" the child, although they probably were not implying Jesus' deity but merely expressing the desire to do homage.

The appearance of heavenly phenomena was commonly thought to announce the birth and death of great people. The Magi, as pagan priests who observed the stars to determine future events or explanations,

CHRISTMAS DAY IS HERE—OR THERE

December 25 probably wasn't the actual day of Jesus' birth. He was likely born in the spring when shepherds watched their flocks nightly (Luke 2:8) because this was the season when lambs might be born. Christians attached their celebration of Christmas to the Roman holiday Saturnalia, in December, because workers were given time off. Surprisingly, even before the Western Church began celebrating Christmas, they celebrated the arrival of the Magi, Christ's manifestation to Gentiles. They called it *Epiphany*, which is an appearance of a deity or insight into reality or truth.

perceived this star as a sign of a Jewish king (see Numbers 24:17, a verse perceived as messianically prophetic). Although Matthew likely would have known the Old Testament forbade astrology (Jeremiah 10:1–2), he did not condemn the Magi. Rather, he contrasted their eagerness to worship Jesus with the Jewish leaders' apathy and Herod's hostility. No longer would God's people be limited to those of Hebrew blood. In the Magi, "all nations" (Matt. 28:19) and people from "the ends of the earth" (Acts 1:8) were already worshiping the new King.

Fearing that the worship of a *born* king would usurp his kingship, Herod called the chief priests (generally Sadducees) and scribes (often Pharisees, scholars who taught and served as experts who interpreted and applied the Old Testament). Herod probably questioned these groups independently of each other to get their reactions, because neither particularly liked him and he might have feared a conspiracy or trick. Note Herod rephrased the Magi's question. He didn't ask the experts to tell him where the "king of the Jews" was to be born, he asked about the Messiah's birth (Matt. 2:4). He was hesitant to even suggest someone else might be king.

The answer to Herod's question, from Micah 5:2, is not an exact quotation of that verse, but the differences are minor, without altering the prophecy or Christ's fulfillment of it. A notable difference is Matthew's image of a "shepherd," implying compassionate guidance and pastoral care. Jesus said of himself, "I am the good shepherd" (John 10:11; see also Hebrews 13:20; 1 Peter 2:25; Revelation 7:17). Contrasted to Herod, Jesus' leadership would be very different.

There were two Bethlehems in Israel—one in Zebulun, seven miles northwest of Nazareth in northern Israel (see Joshua 19:15), and another five miles south of Jerusalem. Jesus' birth was in the southern Bethlehem, called *the city of David* (Luke 2:11) since it was his birthplace and site of his anointing (Ruth 4:17; 1 Samuel 16:1, 12–13).

Herod "secretly" invited the Magi into his presence to link what they saw in the star's appearance with the information of the Jewish experts. Herod instructed them to find the Child and return so he too might pay homage (2:8), a blatant lie.

For the first time, Matthew recorded the star's movement (2:9), leading the Magi from Jerusalem to Bethlehem.[2] The Magi, from a pagan background, were "overjoyed" (2:10). They presented expensive gifts, which were common for royalty, worshiped the Christ-child as a king,

---

COFFEE SHOP CASE STUDY

Rashida works at your local coffee shop and you've developed a healthy friendship with her. Because you bring in your Bible occasionally and treat her respectfully, she's come to suspect you may be a Christian. One day, she sees you reading through this lesson with your Scriptures in hand. She asks, *Are you a Christian?* When you answer affirmatively, she continues: *I've heard many things about Jesus, that he was a moral man, good teacher, and prophet from God. Do you also believe these things, or do you believe something else about him?*

What would you say to her? What are some principles of faith in Jesus Christ you might share?

Here are some to consider:

- Fully God, fully human
- One and equal with God
- Died, buried, and rose again for forgiveness of humanity's sins
- Without error; perfect in all ways
- Fulfilled prophecy
- Only way for salvation and eternity in heaven
- Ascended into heaven, seated at the right hand of God, interceding for those who believe on him as the Son of God

---

and fell to their knees with heads to the ground, demonstrating Eastern protocol when meeting someone who was superior (2:11).[3]

These gift-bearers fulfilled other parts of Old Testament prophecy Matthew didn't mention. Their arrival harkened back to the *streaming of all nations* prophesied 750 years before Christ's birth in Isaiah 2:2–4. Psalm 72:10–15 describes "all kings" falling down before and serving a king, offering gold. Isaiah 60:1–6 says all nations and kings would come offering "gold" and "incense." Literal use of these passages has led to legends and songs identifying the Magi as royalty, and although one carol declares they came from the Orient, their awareness of Jewish messianic expectation is likely from contact with Persia's Jewish community. Persia, thereby, seems a logical place for their origin.

On the Road Again (2:12–15, 19–23)

The Magi's return route changed drastically from the one that brought them after a warning from God (Matt. 2:12). Although they didn't know Herod's true intentions, God certainly did. Thus, rather than returning home via Jerusalem to report to Herod, they "returned . . . by another route." Assuming their homeland was Persia, they possibly returned along a route around the south end of the Dead Sea.

Shortly thereafter, Joseph received another angelic messenger with urgent instructions in a dream (2:13). He was to flee with his family to Egypt, because Herod planned to kill this One born king of the Jews. Certainly Herod confirmed the truth of his negative reputation by ordering the execution of "all the boys in Bethlehem and its vicinity who were two years old and under" (2:16), a choice that defied his claimed conversion to Judaism, both in the brutality of the act and the desire to destroy the long-awaited Messiah. However, he was not the only one who would perceive Jesus as a threat.

The trio left immediately for Egypt (2:14). While it might seem surprising Joseph would rouse a sleeping baby, it was not uncommon to travel at night to avoid the burning heat of the sun and, in this case, the danger of being spotted by Herod's men. The journey of 150–200 miles (depending on the exact border of Egypt at the time) probably took five or ten days. Providentially, the gifts presented by the Magi probably helped finance their trip and survival.

Matthew was most interested in Jesus' return to Israel following the death of Herod, which fulfilled the prophecy of Hosea 11:1. The Book of Hosea pictures God's love for Israel as it recalls the Exodus (Matt. 2:15). After an angel appeared to Joseph a third time, assuring him of their safety, they returned to Israel (2:19–21). The instructions were similar to those previous, "Get up! Take the child and his mother" (2:13, 20), followed by a reason. Joseph's response was equally similar, "So he [Joseph] got up and took the child and his mother" (2:14, 21). Their exile in Egypt likely lasted two to four years; Herod's death was in 4 B.C.. The plural "those" in 2:20 raises some question, but some believe Matthew was comparing Moses' experiences with those of Jesus (see Exodus 4:19). But, it may also refer to Herod's advisors, who, after his death, were no longer in power when his kingdom was divided. His oldest son, Archelaus, ruled in Judea, Samaria, and Idumea. He was notoriously cruel like his father. Herod Antipas, another son, who ruled in Galilee and Perea, was not perceived to be as great a threat. So Joseph, after another warning dream, led the family to their hometown Nazareth in Galilee rather than return to Bethlehem (Matt. 2:22–23).

Once again, Matthew pointed out Jesus' fulfillment of prophecy, but this time he was not specific. No single prophecy foretold that the Messiah would come from Nazareth, but Matthew used a plural, "prophets." He employed a wordplay familiar to his audience (the Hebrew words for *branch* and *Nazareth* share similar roots), who knew quite well that to be called a "Nazarene" was a term of contempt (see John 1:46; 7:52; Acts 24:5). Jesus therefore fulfilled prophecies describing the Messiah as a *Branch* (see Isaiah 11:1; Jer. 23:5; 33:15; Zechariah 3:8) who would be despised (see Pss. 22:6–8; 69:20–21; Isa. 49:7; 53:2–3).

Implications and Actions

Miraculously conceived, Jesus fulfilled Old Testament prophecies so perfectly that his messiahship is undeniable. God preserved Jesus. God sheltered pregnant Mary from stoning and protected the infant Jesus from Herod's attempts to kill him. Angels came to Joseph in dreams presenting messages from God with instruction and warning. A star appeared in the sky prompting extensive travels and worship from astrologers. Through these extraordinary and supernatural circumstances, Jesus' deity was revealed, and his purpose was announced.

Genesis 22:18 promised through Abraham's offspring "all nations" would be blessed; Jesus is that blessing, and his commission is to make disciples of "all nations" (Matt. 28:19). His disciples experience the joy of knowing they serve One who is eternal and omnipotent—God with us. Of the Gospel writers, only Matthew mentioned women in Jesus' genealogy and shared the story of the Magi worshiping the Christ child. This inclusion of women and non-Jewish characters reveals them as valuable in the sight of God and representative of all those to whom the gospel is offered. All are sinners (Romans 3:23) and need Jesus' saving work. He ignores labels of illegitimacy and outcasts and offers his grace to all who would receive it, believe he is worthy, and follow him.

QUESTIONS

1. Considering the risks socially and emotionally, would you have been as obedient to the angel's instructions as Joseph was to follow through with marriage to Mary?

2. God used negative circumstances in the life of Christ (suspicions of his illegitimacy, Herod's determination to murder him) to bring about fulfillment of Scripture. In what circumstances have you seen God bring about fulfillment in your life, professing the truth of Philippians 1:6 and Romans 8:28?

3. Scholars suggest that approximately twenty boys were killed under Herod's command (Matt. 2:16). How do you reconcile this tragedy with your faith?

4. What circumstances surrounding the birth of Jesus draw you to a greater sense of awe or worship? What about those circumstances, for you, makes Jesus more worthy to be followed than anyone else?

5. Will you celebrate Christmas with a deeper understanding or make changes in your methods of celebration as a result of what you've learned today? How?

NOTES

1. The only other occurrences of this title in Matthew are in the Passion narrative, where it is found above Jesus' head on the cross or used by Gentiles as mockery (Matt. 27:11, 29, 37).

2. They naturally assumed the new king would be born in the capital city. Because of popular carols, they are misunderstood to be following the star from their homeland. Matthew only says they saw the star arise.

3. Because three gifts were given, tradition assumes there were three givers, assigned the names Caspar, Melchior, and Balthasar.

MAIN IDEA

Jesus' baptism by John showed Jesus' identification with John's call to genuine repentance in preparation for God's kingdom and brought God's affirmation of Jesus as his beloved Son.

QUESTION TO EXPLORE

What response does Jesus' baptism call for from his disciples?

STUDY AIM

To state what Jesus' baptism by John the Baptist means and identify how it relates to discipleship

QUICK READ

The ministry of John the Baptist and his baptism of Jesus prepared the way for Christ's ministry and modeled the response called for from all Christian disciples.

LESSON TWO
God's Beloved Son, Baptized by John

Gossip in the "fifteenth year of . . . Tiberias Caesar" (Luke 3:1) might have sounded like this: *You should see the clothes he wears and the food he eats. He preaches in the wilderness. People confess their sins and let him baptize them in the river. Did you hear what he said to the Pharisees and Sadducees?*

John the Baptist, a charismatic figure, attracted crowds. Intrigued by his appearance, some people considered him a novelty. For others, his attire and outspokenness piqued contemplation. Some only criticized him. But for others, he offered words of hope they yearned to hear: the Promised One was coming.

MATTHEW 3

¹ In those days John the Baptist came, preaching in the Desert of Judea ² and saying, "Repent, for the kingdom of heaven is near." ³ This is he who was spoken of through the prophet Isaiah:

"A voice of one calling in the desert,
'Prepare the way for the Lord,
make straight paths for him.' "

⁴ John's clothes were made of camel's hair, and he had a leather belt around his waist. His food was locusts and wild honey. ⁵ People went out to him from Jerusalem and all Judea and the whole region of the Jordan. ⁶ Confessing their sins, they were baptized by him in the Jordan River.

⁷ But when he saw many of the Pharisees and Sadducees coming to where he was baptizing, he said to them: "You brood of vipers! Who warned you to flee from the coming wrath? ⁸ Produce fruit in keeping with repentance. ⁹ And do not think you can say to yourselves, 'We have Abraham as our father.' I tell you that out of these stones God can raise up children for Abraham. ¹⁰ The ax is already at the root of the trees, and every tree that does not produce good fruit will be cut down and thrown into the fire.

¹¹ "I baptize you with water for repentance. But after me will come one who is more powerful than I, whose sandals I am not fit to carry. He will baptize you with the Holy Spirit and with fire. ¹² His winnowing fork is in his hand, and he will clear his threshing

floor, gathering his wheat into the barn and burning up the chaff with unquenchable fire."

¹³ Then Jesus came from Galilee to the Jordan to be baptized by John. ¹⁴ But John tried to deter him, saying, "I need to be baptized by you, and do you come to me?"

¹⁵ Jesus replied, "Let it be so now; it is proper for us to do this to fulfill all righteousness." Then John consented.

¹⁶ As soon as Jesus was baptized, he went up out of the water. At that moment heaven was opened, and he saw the Spirit of God descending like a dove and lighting on him. ¹⁷ And a voice from heaven said, "This is my Son, whom I love; with him I am well pleased."

Down By the Riverside (3:1–6)

Skipping over thirty years of Jesus' life, Matthew began this section: "In those days" (Matthew 3:1). He probably meant *in the days Jesus lived at Nazareth* and used the phrase to create transition and indicate historicity. Excepting Luke's description of twelve-year-old Jesus teaching in the temple (Luke 2:41–52), the Scriptures are silent about Jesus' youth and young adulthood. Therefore, we can assume those years of development were exactly that—Jesus' opportunity to grow and mature, but not revealing the fullness of his identity.

By the mid-first century, believers already recognized John the Baptist as Jesus' forerunner (Acts 13:24). John the Baptist's ministry, including his baptism of Jesus, was so significant that all of the Gospel writers included it in their narratives (see Mark 1:1–11; Luke 3:1–22; John 1:19–34). John's title, "the Baptist," was an identifying nickname because of baptism's fundamental role in his ministry. Matthew described John as preaching (*heralding*) a message from God after a prophetic silence of more than 400 years. Not coincidentally, God again spoke to his people in the wilderness. Did God foreordain this setting as a reminder of the forty years their Israelite ancestors wandered in the wilderness after leaving Egypt? John's generation was spiritually wandering (see Matt. 15:7–9). Yet their forefathers had entered the Promised Land, and hope for another promise was "near."

"The wilderness of Judea" included the area west of the Dead Sea. Used as pasture, it was arid but not unpopulated. From 130 B.C. to A.D. 70, a Jewish sect called Essenes lived on the sea's northwest shore in a community called Qumran. Archeological evidence reveals they were an ascetic and communal group who copied and studied Scripture, practiced ritual baptism and strict devotion to God, and emphasized repentance and anticipation of end times. Because John's theology and practices were so similar, some scholars believe he might have lived with the group.

In order to be ready for the promised Messiah, John called the people to repentance (3:2). Unfortunately, the English "repent" does not fully express the meaning of the Greek *metanoeite*, which includes a sense of regret coupled with a fundamental alteration of the entire person and commitment to new behaviors (see Romans 12:2). Repentance is necessary because the kingdom of heaven "has come near." No one knew what to expect from the coming kingdom or the Messiah. Old Testament prophets described the kingdom's dawning with fear and delight (Isaiah 11:1–10; 13:6–9; Ezekiel 30:3; Joel 1—3; Amos 5:18–20; Zephaniah 1—3). Prophecies like these led Jews in the first century to anticipate that Roman rule would be overthrown and Israel's golden age of peace, prosperity, and justice would resume. Therefore, the nearness of the Promised One generated excitement.

Matthew characteristically used Old Testament documentation. Here he used it to support John the Baptist's role (Matt. 3:3). Because of passages like Deuteronomy 18:15–22 and Malachi 3:1, Jews expected a messenger to "prepare the way" for the Messiah's coming. Matthew and John the Baptist himself (John 1:23) interpreted his mission as the "one calling in the desert" to make straight paths for the Lord. This metaphor was easily understood in a culture where roads were often repaired only when royalty was planning to travel them. *Fill up the potholes of sin in your life with repentance,* John proclaimed, *so the path for the Lord's arrival will be a smooth one* (see Isa. 35:8; 40:3). The Messiah purifies, but they must prepare their hearts to receive the Coming One.

Malachi 4:5 promised the messianic forerunner would be the prophet "Elijah," commonly understood as one coming "in the spirit and power of Elijah" (Luke 1:17). John's message not only shared Elijah's zeal; his appearance matched as well (Matt. 3:4). He wore a garment of camel's hair and a leather belt (see 2 Kings 1:8; Zechariah 13:4). The locusts he ate were large grasshoppers, still eaten in the East; perhaps the wild honey helped them go down a little easier. The clothes and diet were of poor people, signifying that neither prophet placed great emphasis on material wealth. Living simply, both Elijah and John demonstrated it's easier to be in right relationship with God when stuff doesn't get in the way (see Matt. 19:24).

Surprisingly, people were not driven away by John's unusual attire and stern message. Rather, crowds came from the entire Jordan River region. Perhaps the experience was like a religious camp or retreat. Since the crowds would have had few distractions, God's message easily pierced hearts ready to listen. Probably stationed at one of the Jordan's fords, John baptized people publicly as a pledge of commitment to change their ways following confession of sin. At the time, baptism (coupled with circumcision) occurred most commonly when Gentiles converted to Judaism, and yet John demanded repentance-based baptism of Jews, too.

I Can't Believe He Said That! (3:7–12)

With notoriety comes criticism, and John received it from the Pharisees and Sadducees, the religious leaders of the day. They came to where he was baptizing (3:7), probably not with open hearts, but instead to evaluate him. While a few may have been sincere, it's improbable many of the religious leaders actually sought repentance-based baptism, or they did so only to fulfill another religious duty (see 6:2, 5, 16). John denounced them in their insincerity. Describing them as vipers implied they were shrewd and dangerous and may have been an allusion to the serpent in Genesis 3. His rhetorical question: "Who warned you . . .?" connotes sarcasm (Matt. 3:7). This challenge was bold in the presence of people who perceived these men to be holy and exemplary leaders. However, it revealed the wrath of God toward hypocrisy.

John followed his accusation with a directive (3:8). He demanded evidence of repentance. John wasn't teaching justification by works; he agreed with Old Testament expectations:

- "The Sovereign LORD says: Repent! Turn from your idols and renounce all your detestable practices!" (Ezek. 14:6).

- "I will judge you, each one according to his ways, declares the Sovereign LORD. Repent! Turn away from all your offenses; then sin will not be your downfall" (Ezek. 18:30).

Passages like these were well known to Pharisees and Sadducees. Still, they mistakenly thought Jewish blood granted them immunity from God's wrath, believing Abraham's righteousness was sufficient. Knowing this, John the Baptist used a play on words ("children" and "stones" are similar in Aramaic), stating that God was able to raise up Jews from them (Matt. 3:9). He was asserting that grace, not race, offers entrance into and secures a place in God's kingdom. Because of their unrighteousness, John likened the religious leaders to an unfruitful tree about to be permanently removed at the roots (3:10).

Water baptism to express a repentant heart is good, John continued (3:11), but it was merely preparatory. Jesus would come, baptizing "with the Holy Spirit and with fire" to purify and refine believers. Many Jews believed the Spirit had been withdrawn until the Messiah arrived, and so this announcement would have generated excitement. Jesus, John implied, is the Coming One (Psalms 118:26; 40:7) who is worthy to perform this baptism. In spite of John the Baptist's popularity, he humbly

SOAKING WET

Traditionally, Baptist theology denotes baptism as a practice called an ordinance, an act of obedience commissioned by Christ (Matt. 4:17) but not necessary for salvation. Additionally, this ordinance is executed through immersion, not sprinkling, because the root of the Greek word used by the writers of the New Testament carries the connotation of dipping or submersion.

Occasionally, re-baptism occurs in believer's lives, usually because they aren't convinced their first baptism followed a genuine conversion experience, or because they want to make a public statement of recommitment to their faith in Christ. Regardless, it serves as a primary step of discipleship.

The autonomy of individual Baptist churches affords the opportunity to develop practices and principles relative to baptism and church membership. What are the traditions and practices of your local church body regarding baptism?

(see John 3:30) insisted he was not fit to carry the Messiah's sandals, a task reserved for the lowliest servants.

John stated Jesus would perform an additional task (Matt. 3:12). A winnowing fork, an image familiar to those who heard his message, was used to toss wheat and chaff into the wind. The lighter chaff blew away from the heavier wheat as both fell to the ground. The threshing floor was then cleared by gathering the wheat for storage and bundling the chaff for fuel. Those not found to be wheat in Jesus' hand would experience the "unquenchable fire" of judgment (see Isa. 66:24; Matt. 23:33; Mark 9:43; Revelation 20:15).

Right(eous) in the Center of God's Will (3:13–17)

During John's ministry, Jesus surprised John by traveling more than 150 miles to be baptized by him (Matt. 3:13). John knew Jesus was decidely different from the others he baptized, and so he struggled to comprehend why Jesus needed to be baptized (3:14). Earlier, the Pharisees and Sadducees were unworthy of John's baptism, and now he believed his baptism unworthy of Jesus.

To John's hesitancy, Jesus answered with messianic authority: "let it be so now" (3:15). "It [was] proper" because it obediently accomplished God's will. Why did God demand Jesus' baptism by John? No prophecies or commandments insisted the Messiah be baptized. Instead, the sacrifice of what Jesus has died to—the use of his deity for his own advantage (Philippians 2:6)—is his righteous act of obedience. Baptism symbolized Jesus' choice to live as humanity, relying on the Holy Spirit. Furthermore, Jesus' baptism endorsed John's message as divinely ordained, and by revealing Jesus as the Messiah (John 1:31), marked the transition from John's ministry to Jesus'.

Christian baptism is an act of obedience (see small article, "Soaking Wet"). It symbolizes a Christian disciple's prior cleansing by repentance and forgiveness of sins, death to old ways of life, and a new abundant life with Christ. Jesus' baptism foreshadowed his own burial and resurrection (see Rom. 6:1–7). Immersion reflects Christ's burial and resurrection.

Because Jesus acted in obedience, the Spirit of God descended like a dove (Matt. 3:16). "Heaven was opened" is an Old Testament phrase (Ezek. 1:1), implying divine work. While it could mean the Spirit

A PRACTICAL GUIDEBOOK

Matthew wrote his Gospel to serve as a lifestyle and faith guide for converts. He began with historical validation of Jesus' messiahship but then recorded Jesus' life and ministry as a model for believers to emulate. Make a list of the suggested helps you find in this chapter. Here are a few to consider:

- Repent (3:2)
- Respond to the Lord's work (3:3)
- Be baptized (3:6)
- Live what you say you believe (3:8)
- Avoid unrighteous life choices (3:8,10)
- Receive the Holy Spirit's presence (3:11)
- Don't try to deter God's work (3:14)
- Obey, even when it seems strange (3:15)

descended like a dove (*peacefully, gently*), Luke 3:22 indicates the dove came in "bodily form." In Jewish tradition, doves symbolized an end of judgment and the beginning of blessing. In this act, the One who would baptize with the Spirit experienced a formal anointing to empower the accomplishment of his mission. It also served as an inauguration of Jesus' ministry, much like a servant's commissioning or king's coronation. And what better comparisons? He is the Suffering Servant (Isa. 53:11) and King of kings (Rev. 17:14; 19:16)!

Each person of the Trinity is represented in this brief passage. With the dove came the Spirit's outpouring. The deity of Jesus was revealed by the "voice from heaven," an identifier of divinity, that is, God himself. God expressed "love" (Greek *agapetos*), an emotional and affectionate term meaning *chosen*, and also *pleasure* ("well pleased," Greek *eudokesa*), a word indicating God's eternal delight in Jesus. Jesus' status remained unchanged (he was already the Son; see Ps. 2:7; Isa. 42:1), and yet this scene identified him as the Messiah. Thus, Jesus' baptism demonstrated how disciples can live righteously: by the Spirit's power and by God's word (Acts 1:8; Matt. 4:4).

Implications and Actions

John's ministry as forerunner prepared hearts to receive the Messiah's work. John encouraged the Jews of his day to repent so they might be ready to receive the righteousness Jesus offered. The message expanded to include the Gentiles, however, people who formerly were excluded from the kingdom of God. Yet, the Pharisees and Sadducees, who thought themselves securely placed in the kingdom, were in fact trusting in the wrong thing—their ancestral heritage—to merit their salvation.

Unfortunately, people today make similar assumptions. Those who have been baptized (either as infants or unbelieving adults) often think their eternal destination is secure. Still others think church membership or position, a Christian family, moral living, or lip-service to repentance and trust in Christ are sufficient. Yet evidence of a changed life is the marker of faith (James 2:18).

Jesus' baptism, while not necessary to reveal a heart of repentance, revealed his submission to God's desire for every aspect of his life, even to the point of death on a cross (Phil. 2:6–8). Jesus' followers who follow this act in obedience are choosing to reveal themselves as his disciples.

QUESTIONS

1. What do you think your response would have been to John the Baptist? Would you have even gone to hear him? Would you have been a dispassionate observer, a curious follower, a critic, or a disciple? Why?

2. Is there a particular part of John's simple message, "Repent, for the kingdom of heaven is near" (3:2), that resonates with you? If so, what is it and why?

3. Relate John's words in Matthew 3:9 to the statement, *God has no grandchildren.*

4. Jesus said John should baptize him "to fulfill all righteousness" (3:15). It was a simple answer to John's question, but it was satisfactory enough for John. If Jesus said that to you, would it be sufficient, or do you demand detailed descriptions of his plan before you'll follow in obedience?

5. If you have not been baptized, why not? How can you "fulfill all righteousness" if you have already been baptized?

FOCAL TEXT
Matthew 4:12–22

BACKGROUND
Matthew 4:12–25

MAIN IDEA
Jesus changed the disciples'
lives when they responded
to his call, "Follow me."

QUESTION TO EXPLORE
What kind of response
does Jesus' challenge,
"Follow me," call for?

STUDY AIM
To decide how I will respond
to Jesus' ministry in light of
the response of disciples whom
he challenged, "Follow me"

QUICK READ
Jesus fulfilled prophecy as
he ministered throughout
Galilee, calling people to
repentance and the challenge
of following him as disciples.

LESSON THREE

*Called to
Follow Jesus*

Up to this point in Matthew's Gospel, it's all been prologue. The first three chapters reveal Jesus as the Messiah who fulfilled Scripture, foreshadow Jesus' acceptance by Gentiles and the rejection of Jesus by his own people, and introduce Jesus' mission through John the Baptist's ministry and the baptism of Jesus. But for Matthew, the story had only begun. He knew Jesus' ministry would soon change the lives of those he encountered, and ultimately the world, when people responded to three simple words: "Come, follow me" (Matthew 4:19).

MATTHEW 4:12–22

[12] When Jesus heard that John had been put in prison, he returned to Galilee. [13] Leaving Nazareth, he went and lived in Capernaum, which was by the lake in the area of Zebulun and Naphtali— [14] to fulfill what was said through the prophet Isaiah:
[15] "Land of Zebulun and land of Naphtali,
    the way to the sea, along the Jordan,
    Galilee of the Gentiles—
[16] the people living in darkness
    have seen a great light;
on those living in the land of the shadow of death
    a light has dawned."
[17] From that time on Jesus began to preach, "Repent, for the kingdom of heaven is near."
[18] As Jesus was walking beside the Sea of Galilee, he saw two brothers, Simon called Peter and his brother Andrew. They were casting a net into the lake, for they were fishermen. [19] "Come, follow me," Jesus said, "and I will make you fishers of men." [20] At once they left their nets and followed him.
[21] Going on from there, he saw two other brothers, James son of Zebedee and his brother John. They were in a boat with their father Zebedee, preparing their nets. Jesus called them, [22] and immediately they left the boat and their father and followed him.

Bad News, Good News (4:12–16)

Following the delight of Jesus' baptism (Matt. 3:13–17) and the challenges of the wilderness temptations (4:1–11), Jesus received some bad news. His cousin, fellow minister, and prophetic forerunner, John the Baptist, had been put into prison (4:12), where he would remain until his execution. This completed John's work as the forerunner, and the One to whom he pointed would now arise (John 3:29–31). Why John the Baptist's imprisonment prompted Jesus' return to Galilee is uncertain, but it was obvious to Matthew that Jesus' actions were the fulfillment of Scripture.

According to Luke 4:16–31, Jesus went first to his hometown of Nazareth but left after a violent response to his teaching in the synagogue. Avoiding the attempt to murder him, Jesus went northeast to the city of Capernaum to continue his work (Matt. 4:13).

Jesus' ministry had a unique opportunity to grow in Capernaum. In Jerusalem, he would have had to contend with the opposition of religious leaders. Unlike Nazareth's population, Capernaum's residents had not known him from childhood and probably had few, if any, pre-conceived ideas about him. Located on the northwest shore of the Sea of Galilee, Capernaum was a center of Galilean political life, enjoying a thriving fishing industry. It was an ideal home base for Jesus' ministry because of its size and significance. The city served as home for some of the disciples: brothers James and John, and also Peter and Andrew, who were originally from Bethsaida (John 1:44) but had moved to Capernaum (Mark 1:21, 29).

Matthew's description of Capernaum as "by the lake in the area of Zebulun and Naphtali" (Matt. 4:13) reflects the prophecy from Isaiah 9:1–2, which he referenced in the next verses (Matt. 4:15–16). Zebulun (where Nazareth lies) and Naphtali (where Capernaum lies) were the Old Testament territories of Galilee. The prophecy was originally spoken in reference to a deliverer for Israel from Assyrian oppression. Matthew applied Isaiah's words to Jesus' messianic work of deliverance, bringing to complete fulfillment Isaiah's expectation.

The "way of the sea" (4:15) was a Roman road connecting Damascus (northeast of Galilee) with Caesarea on the western Mediterranean coast. Part of the road passed along the Sea of Galilee through Capernaum and Bethsaida, another key city in Jesus' ministry.

Beyond "the Jordan" lay the Decapolis region, to which Jesus' ministry also extended, further fulfilling this prophecy. "Galilee of the Gentiles" was a common designation for the entire northern Sea of Galilee region because it historically (even in Isaiah's day) had a large Gentile population and in the first century had a large Gentile population as well.

Matthew's choice to include this passage foreshadowed the ministry Jesus and his followers would have to Gentile nations (Matt. 8:10; 15:2–28; 24:14; 28:19). Yet the word Matthew used for "people" in 4:16 often refers to Israel specifically, rather than humanity in general. Thus understood, "the people living in darkness," are Jewish. Frustrated and despairing, dwelling among pagans who mocked God and persecuted their faith and lifestyle, they were nevertheless given hope, "a great light," which is the fulfillment of God's promises—the Messiah (see Luke 1:78–79; John 1:4–5, 9; 8:12).

Those "living in the land of the shadow of death" lived where the darkness was most dense, and yet it was here the light "dawned." The light of Jesus' teaching came first from this region (see Psalm 119:105,130).

Same Song, Second Verse (4:17)

Twice in his Gospel, Matthew used the phrase "from that time on" to introduce new segments of narration. Here it prefaced Jesus' work, ministry, and teaching, and in 16:21, it marked the commencement of events leading to the cross and resurrection.

Jesus began his teaching and healing ministry by repeating what John preached: "Repent, for the kingdom of heaven is near." Jesus' meaning was also the same. "Repent" means not just feeling sorry or changing your mind, but altering your actions. This message was not original to them. Old Testament prophets such as Isaiah (Isaiah 59:20), Jeremiah (Jeremiah 15:19), Ezekiel (Ezekiel 14:6; 18:30, 32), and Hosea (Hosea 11:5) begged God's people centuries earlier to repent by transforming their hearts and behaviors.

Like John, Jesus perceived repentance as a pressing matter because the kingdom of heaven is nearby. The kingdom is God's sovereignty over all creation wherein redeemed people and nature exist in harmony and holiness. Elsewhere in the New Testament, the term *kingdom of God* is used, but the phrases are equivalent (see Matt. 19:23–24; Mark 10:23–25).

"Kingdom of heaven" does not restrict God's reign to heaven (see Ps. 135:6; Matt.11:25; Acts 17:24). Rather, it reflects the Jewish tradition of avoiding the use of God's name so as not to use it in vain and violate the third commandment (Exodus 20:7). Furthermore, Matthew's use of "kingdom of heaven" anticipates Christ's authority following his resurrection (Philippians 2:9–11).

From this point forward, Matthew's narrative would expose the religious leaders' growing animosity toward Jesus as they wrestled for control of the people's hearts and minds. Simultaneously, Jesus' popularity among the people would grow because of his healing work and unusual teachings. Crowds would follow Jesus' ministry, but it would start with a few whom he invited, saying, "Come, follow me" (Matt. 4:19).

Follow the Leader (4:18–22)

What kinds of invitations make you drop everything and go? Does it matter who's asking? Are you an immediate responder, or do you think things through first? What motivates a change in your plans?

After John's imprisonment, it was only natural for Peter to resume his life and work as a fisherman at the Sea of Galilee (see John 1:40–42). That was where Jesus found him and his brother. They weren't doing anything unique or spectacular. Yet their lives were about to make a radical change.

Matthew, still guided by the Isaiah passage quoted in verses 15–16, noted that Jesus was "beside the Sea of Galilee" (Matt. 4:18). Brothers Simon Peter and Andrew were casting a net over their shoulders, spreading it into a circle to target specific areas for catching fish. The word for their net suggests a net for casting on both sides of the boat and not a dragnet. This type of fishing is significant, for it indicates they were casting in a specific area, for a specific target. That's exactly what Jesus was about to ask them do, although the target would not be fish, but people.

"Come, follow me" is literally, *come after me* (4:19). "Come" can even be read as an interjection with an exclamation mark. This sense of urgency is rooted in the nearness of the kingdom (4:17). By joining Jesus, the fishermen's new work would be to fish for people by calling them to repentance so they, too, would be ready for the kingdom of heaven.

These professional fishermen knew their work was exhausting, time-consuming, and messy. Jesus' call to fish for people would be equally challenging. The new followers would quickly see they must *fish* in difficult circumstances—when weary, against opposition, and even to the point of personal loss and sacrifice (see 5:11; 10:37; 16:24; Mark 6:30–32).

The Greek language actually has several expressions for *following*, but all imply a physical act. Walking while teaching was characteristic for rabbis (teachers) and philosophers of the period. This practice enabled students to absorb the instruction and imitate their master's example, which they were to pass along to others.

Unfortunately, the uniqueness of Jesus' calling is lost to most modern-day readers. First-century traveling rabbis did not seek out students. Rather, individuals desiring tutelage initiated a relationship with the master, requesting training. Conversely, Jesus hand-picked his disciples (meaning *pupils*), and as they followed him around in his travels and ministry, he equipped them to fulfill their calling in this new work (see

APOSTLE OR DISCIPLE?

What, if any, is the difference between an *apostle* and a *disciple*?

Although some Christian faith practices or denominations use the expression *apostle* to describe their church leadership, traditionally the term is reserved for those who witnessed Jesus in his physical resurrected form, accepted him as the Son of God, proclaimed the gospel, and served in roles of leadership and authority in the first-century church. Jesus called his twelve disciples "apostles" (Luke 6:13) and commissioned them to preach the coming of the kingdom, cast out demons, and heal diseases (Matt. 10:1; Luke 9:2).

A Christian disciple, in contrast, is anyone who is a follower of Jesus and his teachings, believing by faith that Jesus is the sinless, risen Son of God who died for the sins of humanity. True disciples desire to be obedient to Jesus, believing that the goal of their discipleship is righteousness. They are people from any walk of life, commissioned by Jesus to be representatives of Jesus and his grace.

Mark 13:11; Luke 12:11–12). In Luke's account, he revealed Jesus' ability to provide for their needs by coupling the event of their calling with a miraculous catch of fish (Luke 5:1–11).

The parallel for today's disciples is clear. Jesus' calling to "follow me" extends to all, and he demands discipleship as a lifelong commitment to obeying God's will. He will equip (Matt. 28:19–20; Acts 1:8; 2 Corinthians 3:6, Colossians 1:12) and provide (Ephesians 2:10; Phil. 4:19) for his followers, but they are to live in community with one another. Jesus could have individually walked with each disciple to invest himself in them, but he didn't. He called them to join a group, to journey through life together. So important was that point to Matthew that Matthew was the only Gospel writer to include the church in his narrative (Matt. 16:18; 18:17).

A second pair of brothers were "preparing their nets" (4:21), which makes it seem they were getting started for the day. The verb, however, means *mend*. James and John most likely were making repairs after a night's fishing. The Gospel of Mark tells us their boat was big enough to include hired workers (Mark 1:19–20), which may indicate they had an extensive and financially successful operation.

Matthew highlighted the brothers' immediate responses ("at once" in 4:20 and "immediately" in 4:22) because he recognized true discipleship: unhesitatingly abandoning the past to follow unconditionally. Peter and Andrew left their nets. John and James left their boat, their father, and perhaps a lucrative lifestyle and business. They left it all to do one simple thing: to follow Jesus. Will we?

Implications and Actions

Jesus' first call is to repentance. He is the light that dawned to bring hope to humanity's sinful condition. Have you answered this call? Are your life, mind, and heart daily being renewed (Romans 12:1–2)? Is your repentance not just once for eternal salvation, but moment-by-moment, interacting with him for cleansing from sin?

Second, Jesus calls us to discipleship. For the first disciples and for us, it is a matter of costly obedience. Matthew's audience was certainly aware they lived under threat of danger or death, and with the exception of the Apostle John, most, if not all, of Jesus' closest friends likely would

AM I FOLLOWING JESUS?

Consider your honest answer to these questions:

- Have I repented of my sins and sought Jesus' forgiveness and leadership?
- Am I living in willful sin? (Consider the media you ingest; compare it with Phil. 4:8.)
- Am I committed to spiritual growth, worship, and prayer? privately? with my local church family?
- Is the Holy Spirit free to work in and through me?
- Is my life an example of purity and integrity?
- Am I boldly speaking the truth of the gospel to those who need to hear it?
- Am I actively looking for opportunities to minister and serve others?

be martyred. To follow Jesus means leaving behind personal preferences and agendas, breaking from the past, and fundamentally reshaping our priorities, not out of obligation, but because of love for him.

Jesus also expects his disciples to call others to repentance and fellowship. Are you inviting others to experience this kind of relationship with him? Or is your message and example of discipleship a religion of rules to follow, instead of an actual dialogue with Christ every moment of every day?

QUESTIONS

1. What difference does it make that Jesus fulfilled Old Testament prophecies?

2. Human nature seems to clamor for the latest new book, the most novel ideas. Why do you think Jesus repeated John's words: "Repent, for the kingdom of heaven has come near," instead of having a new and different message?

3. Do you perceive discipleship as complying with a list of rules or living in a moment-by-moment relationship with Jesus? Why? Is there something you need to do to reshape or refocus your perspective?

4. Mending their nets for the next cast at sea, John and James left potential profit to follow Jesus. What will you leave or have you left behind to follow him? Financial gain, security in your life, status and comfort of your family? Something else?

5. How do you think the father of James and John felt about their choice to follow Jesus?

Learning from Jesus

Unit two, "Learning from Jesus," consists of five lessons that emphasize instructions for disciples. These lessons study Jesus' teachings on discipleship in Matthew 5—7, generally known as the Sermon on the Mount. One commentator on these chapters refers to these chapters as Jesus' "Discourse on Discipleship." [1]

NOTES

1. R.T. France, *The Gospel of Matthew*, The New International Commentary on the New Testament (Grand Rapids, Michigan: William B. Eerdmans Publishing Company, 2007), see on Matthew 5:1—7:29 introduction.

FOCAL TEXT
Matthew 5:1–16

BACKGROUND
Matthew 5:1–16

MAIN IDEA
Distinctive qualities and actions are to characterize Jesus' disciples.

QUESTION TO EXPLORE
How is living an ordinary human life different from living as a disciple of Jesus?

STUDY AIM
To lead the group to identify distinctive qualities and actions of Jesus' disciples and to evaluate their lives by them

QUICK READ
The Sermon on the Mount has been referred to as the essence of the Christian way of life, a way of life marked by distinctive qualities and actions.

LESSON FOUR

The Distinctive Life of Disciples

The word *disciple* and the word *discipline* come from the same root word. The word *discipline* means to do what one is supposed to do when one is supposed to do it. A *disciple* is one who does what he or she is supposed to do when he or she is supposed to do it. The Sermon on the Mount is a manual of spiritual disciplines that are to shape the life of the disciple. They are not ordinary qualities and actions but supernatural qualities and actions.

Discipline involves some basic instructions and some deliberate actions. The legendary UCLA basketball coach, John Wooden, began each season with basic instructions to his athletes on how to put on their socks. Wooden said that the reason he did this was to keep his players from getting blisters that would in turn hinder them from running, jumping, and giving their best effort. He wanted their minds to be on the basketball game and not on the pain of blistered feet.[1]

In the Sermon on the Mount, recorded in Matthew 5—7, Jesus gave his disciples some basic instructions about their relationship to God expressed in some deliberate actions. He wanted their minds to be on the kingdom of God.

MATTHEW 5:1–16

[1] Now when he saw the crowds, he went up on a mountainside and sat down. His disciples came to him, [2] and he began to teach them, saying:
   [3] "Blessed are the poor in spirit,
        for theirs is the kingdom of heaven.
   [4] Blessed are those who mourn,
        for they will be comforted.
   [5] Blessed are the meek,
        for they will inherit the earth.
   [6] Blessed are those who hunger and thirst for righteousness,
        for they will be filled.
   [7] Blessed are the merciful,
        for they will be shown mercy.
   [8] Blessed are the pure in heart,
        for they will see God.

> [9] Blessed are the peacemakers,
>   for they will be called sons of God.
> [10] Blessed are those who are persecuted because of righteousness,
>   for theirs is the kingdom of heaven.
> [11] "Blessed are you when people insult you, persecute you and falsely say all kinds of evil against you because of me. [12] Rejoice and be glad, because great is your reward in heaven, for in the same way they persecuted the prophets who were before you.
> [13] "You are the salt of the earth. But if the salt loses its saltiness, how can it be made salty again? It is no longer good for anything, except to be thrown out and trampled by men.
> [14] "You are the light of the world. A city on a hill cannot be hidden. [15] Neither do people light a lamp and put it under a bowl. Instead they put it on its stand, and it gives light to everyone in the house. [16] In the same way, let your light shine before men, that they may see your good deeds and praise your Father in heaven.

The Blessing of the Disciplined Life (5:1–10)

The common method of travel in Jesus' day was walking. Often a Jewish rabbi would walk along a road reading or engaged in conversation with his students or disciples. But when he was officially teaching, he would always sit. The preacher in the synagogue would sit to deliver his message. Universities and seminaries often raise money to endow a *chair* in some field of study. The *chair* represents the place a professor sat to deliver his lectures. Even today when the Pope makes an official announcement or pronounces a new law, he speaks *ex cathedra*, meaning *out from the throne where he sits*. So when Matthew wrote that Jesus "sat down" as he began to teach, we can ascertain that Jesus was taking the posture of one giving an official teaching (Matthew 5:1). He was prepared to teach his disciples the essence of living as one of his disciples.

The Sermon on the Mount opens with eight qualities of the character of a disciple. They have been called *The Beatitudes* from the Latin word *beatus*, meaning *blessed*. The word *blessed* describes an inner joy

BLESSED

The English word *blessed* is a translation of the Greek word *makarios*. It can be translated *blessed, fortunate,* or *happy.* The Old Testament equivalent of the Greek *makarios* is *asheri,* found in Psalm 1. It is an intensive Hebrew verb and can be translated *oh, how happy!* This word denotes a person who is living a spiritually disciplined life that settles him or her within the deepest part of his or her being. The person is very happy or satisfied as a result of the spiritually disciplined life.

that cannot be taken away by the world. It is more than happiness. The word *happiness* is built on the root *hap*, which means *chance*. Human happiness is often dependent on chances over which a person has no control. Many things, such as illness, accidents, or death, can change happiness into sorrow. But the blessing rooted in one's relationship with God cannot be taken away.

Our natural way of thinking would probably not consider the eight qualities of the Beatitudes as blessings. What person would think that being poor in spirit, mourning, being meek, hungering and thirsting, being merciful, being pure in heart, being peacemakers, or being per-secuted would lead to a blessed and happy life? Obviously, the natural man would reject these qualities outright as leading to blessedness or happiness.

The Beatitudes reverse what might ordinarily be expected to occur. The opposite of "poor in spirit" is *proud in spirit.* The opposite of "mourn" is *being uncaring* or *seeking pleasure.* The opposite of the "meek" are the *aggressors.* The opposite of the "persecuted" are *those who play it safe, who compromise, or who never take a stand for what is right.* Are these qualities that produce blessing and happiness?

How would these eight qualities in the life of the disciple look today? The "poor in spirit" are those who are not satisfied with themselves but are always looking to live like Jesus. "Those who mourn" are the ones whose sorrow drives them into a deeper, loving relationship with friends and God. The "meek" have learned that submitting to the will of God is a better way to live happily. "Those who hunger and thirst after righteousness" have a desire to live a fruitful life in God's kingdom. A "merciful" person is ready to help those in trouble, overlooking the little things and forgiving the large things. The "pure in heart" are people of honesty and integrity. What one sees on the outside is what resides on the inside. The "peacemaker" is more than a peacekeeper or peace-lover. A "peacemaker" is someone who helps knit people together. To be "persecuted because of righteousness" means to be hounded or harassed because of living up to God's standards. These are distinctive qualities and actions that should characterize Jesus' disciples.

The Difficulty of the Disciplined Life (5:11–12)

Jesus did not want to mislead his disciples about the difficulty of the disciplined life. He taught them clearly that living righteously would bring "insult," "false persecution," and "all kinds of evil accusations" (5:11).

The Greek root word for persecution, *dioko*, means *to pursue*. It means *to hound someone or to harass someone*. The pursuit Jesus described was a pursuit to insult or to falsely say all kinds of evil against the disciple. This kind of persecution was an attempt to intimidate a disciple for refusing to be compliant with worldly standards or for refusing to go along with what is wrong.

Persecution comes from the activities of the disciplined life—living righteously. Jesus did not teach his disciples to go out of their way to create persecution but to expect persecution because of their righteous way of life.

Peter, one of Jesus' first disciples, learned about this persecution in his own life. He wrote in 1 Peter 4:15–16, "If you suffer, it should not be as a murderer or thief or any other kind of criminal, or even as a meddler. However, if you suffer as a Christian, do not be ashamed, but praise God that you bear that name."

The practical kind of righteousness found in the eight Beatitudes will bring persecution from a culture dominated by other religions or secularism, both of which are hostile to Jesus. Peter wrote again in 1 Peter 2:19–21,

> For it is commendable if a man bears up under the pain of unjust suffering because he is conscious of God. But how is

it to your credit if you receive a beating for doing wrong and endure it? But if you suffer for doing good and you endure it, this is commendable before God. To this you were called, because Christ suffered for you, leaving you an example that you should follow in his steps.

Persecution will come to every faithful disciple of Jesus in some form. God had only one Son without sin, but none without suffering.

The difficulty of the disciplined life brings a twofold blessing: "the kingdom of heaven" and "a great reward in heaven" (Matt. 5:10, 12). When one stands up under suffering and does not back away from the will of God for his or her life, the kingdom of heaven becomes a reality in the person's life. "The kingdom of heaven" means *the rule of God* in one's life. This is life lived at the highest level. Such a life provides a sense of spiritual satisfaction that is called *blessed*. When one makes the tough and disciplined choices for the right reasons, there is an accompanying sense of satisfaction.

The disciplined life is difficult but blessed!

The Influence of the Disciplined Life (5:13–16)

Every disciple is expected to have a godly influence in this world. Jesus states emphatically, *You all ARE the salt of the earth and the light of the world* (5:13–14). He did not say *one of you might be* the salt of the earth, but *you all are* the salt of the earth and *you all are* the light of the world. There are no other options. The distinctive qualities and actions found in the Beatitudes are like salt and light.

Jesus described his disciples as "a city on a hill" (5:14). They were occupying a prominent position in the world. They were occupying that position not of their own will but by the will of God. They were in that prominent position to influence other people to see life from God's perspective. The disciple of Jesus Christ is placed in a prominent and influential position by the sovereign will of God. Nations come and go. Governments come and go. Organizations come and go. But the disciple of Jesus Christ stands as "a city on a hill."

Salt and light are powerful metaphors for the influence disciples are to exert on the world around them. Salt was valuable as a preservative and

MERCY

Bobby was taking his family to breakfast on a Saturday morning. It was cold and rainy on the outside but warm on the inside of Bobby's SUV. His son and daughter were chatting happily in the back seat, excited to be going to their favorite restaurant with dad and mom. Brad, Bobby's son, asked his dad what kind of pancakes he would order from the restaurant. Bobby stopped at a busy intersection while mulling over his answer. The family's attention was drawn to a disheveled woman, standing on the curb, with a small child standing next to her, holding a sign that read, "Homeless—hungry—Will you help?" Bobby knew his entire family saw the woman, her daughter, and the sign. Bobby is a Christian. How should he respond to this situation?

for seasoning meat. Salt was so valuable that Roman soldiers in the first century were often paid a salary in salt. The light was valuable for guiding one on a journey or for helping make visible that which was clouded in darkness.

The distinctive qualities and actions of the disciple described by Jesus function as a visible manifestation of the influence of salt and light. Living the blessed life publicly exerts a positive and hopeful influence in a degenerate and darkened world. These distinctive qualities help preserve spiritual life and give spiritual guidance.

Implications and Actions

It is important to note that this sermon was not given to the multitudes but to Jesus' disciples. This Sermon on the Mount probably followed soon after the choosing of the twelve disciples. The teaching followed the choosing. Some people think of Jesus as a great teacher, but if one does not know Jesus as Savior first, his teachings can be beyond understanding and can lead to despair. One becomes changed by Jesus rather than by his teachings, and then Jesus' teachings shape the distinctive qualities and actions that characterize the lives of his disciples.

To detach the disciplines of the Christian life from the profession of the Christian faith is to make the Christian faith irrelevant. The seemingly impossible ethic of the Beatitudes helps to focus us away from ourselves and toward God. In moving us toward God, we find a blessedness that could never be achieved by human effort.

QUESTIONS

1. What is the basic difference between *blessed* and *happy*?

2. Why would Jesus address his disciples directly and the crowd indirectly?

3. Which of the Beatitudes speak most pointedly to you today?

4. How does a disciple influence the world as salt and light without being *bossy* or *legalistic*?

NOTES

1. http://newsroom.ucla.edu/portal/ucla/wooden-shoes-and-socks-84177.aspx. Accessed 7/15/11.

LESSON FIVE
Live By Jesus' Interpretation of God's Will

FOCAL TEXT
Matthew 5:17–48

BACKGROUND
Matthew 5:17–48

MAIN IDEA
Jesus instructs his disciples to live a life of complete goodness springing from a heart grounded in the character of God.

QUESTION TO EXPLORE
How can a life of discipleship be measured?

STUDY AIM
To decide how I will respond to Jesus' interpretation of God's will

QUICK READ
The will of God as interpreted by Jesus demands a positive and constructive lifestyle based on an inward spiritual motivation. This inward spiritual motivation comes from a heart grounded in the character of God.

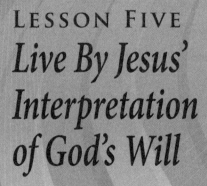

Long distance runners sometimes experience a *runner's high* when they are more than half way through their run. The *runner's high* is a sense of euphoria that allows the runner to run almost effortlessly with renewed energy. After training for an event, a runner gives his or her best effort according to the rules that provide guidance for a successful endeavor. They do what they can, according to their training. But, when the *runner's high* kicks in, they are able to do what they can't. Their bodies move beyond simple mechanics to a higher level of performance.

Jesus interpreted God's will for the Mosaic law by fulfilling it and going beyond it. He taught that a life of discipleship can be measured by how a disciple goes beyond the simple mechanics of the Mosaic law to live a life of goodness springing from a heart grounded in the character of God.

MATTHEW 5:17–48

[17] "Do not think that I have come to abolish the Law or the Prophets; I have not come to abolish them but to fulfill them. [18] I tell you the truth, until heaven and earth disappear, not the smallest letter, not the least stroke of a pen, will by any means disappear from the Law until everything is accomplished. [19] Anyone who breaks one of the least of these commandments and teaches others to do the same will be called least in the kingdom of heaven, but whoever practices and teaches these commands will be called great in the kingdom of heaven. [20] For I tell you that unless your righteousness surpasses that of the Pharisees and the teachers of the law, you will certainly not enter the kingdom of heaven.

[21] "You have heard that it was said to the people long ago, 'Do not murder, and anyone who murders will be subject to judgment.' [22] But I tell you that anyone who is angry with his brother will be subject to judgment. Again, anyone who says to his brother, 'Raca,' is answerable to the Sanhedrin. But anyone who says, 'You fool!' will be in danger of the fire of hell.

[23] "Therefore, if you are offering your gift at the altar and there remember that your brother has something against you, [24] leave your gift there in front of the altar. First go and be reconciled to your brother; then come and offer your gift.

25 "Settle matters quickly with your adversary who is taking you to court. Do it while you are still with him on the way, or he may hand you over to the judge, and the judge may hand you over to the officer, and you may be thrown into prison. 26 I tell you the truth, you will not get out until you have paid the last penny.

27 "You have heard that it was said, 'Do not commit adultery.' 28 But I tell you that anyone who looks at a woman lustfully has already committed adultery with her in his heart. 29 If your right eye causes you to sin, gouge it out and throw it away. It is better for you to lose one part of your body than for your whole body to be thrown into hell. 30 And if your right hand causes you to sin, cut it off and throw it away. It is better for you to lose one part of your body than for your whole body to go into hell.

31 "It has been said, 'Anyone who divorces his wife must give her a certificate of divorce.' 32 But I tell you that anyone who divorces his wife, except for marital unfaithfulness, causes her to become an adulteress, and anyone who marries the divorced woman commits adultery.

33 "Again, you have heard that it was said to the people long ago, 'Do not break your oath, but keep the oaths you have made to the Lord.' 34 But I tell you, Do not swear at all: either by heaven, for it is God's throne; 35 or by the earth, for it is his footstool; or by Jerusalem, for it is the city of the Great King. 36 And do not swear by your head, for you cannot make even one hair white or black. 37 Simply let your 'Yes' be 'Yes,' and your 'No,' 'No'; anything beyond this comes from the evil one.

38 "You have heard that it was said, 'Eye for eye, and tooth for tooth.' 39 But I tell you, Do not resist an evil person. If someone strikes you on the right cheek, turn to him the other also. 40 And if someone wants to sue you and take your tunic, let him have your cloak as well. 41 If someone forces you to go one mile, go with him two miles. 42 Give to the one who asks you, and do not turn away from the one who wants to borrow from you.

43 "You have heard that it was said, 'Love your neighbor and hate your enemy.' 44 But I tell you: Love your enemies and pray for those who persecute you, 45 that you may be sons of your

Father in heaven. He causes his sun to rise on the evil and the good, and sends rain on the righteous and the unrighteous. [46] If you love those who love you, what reward will you get? Are not even the tax collectors doing that? [47] And if you greet only your brothers, what are you doing more than others? Do not even pagans do that? [48] Be perfect, therefore, as your heavenly Father is perfect.

God's Will Goes Beyond the Mosaic Law

Jesus did not come "to abolish" the Mosaic law but "to fulfill it" (Matthew 5:17). He emphasized the importance of the Mosaic law by saying that "not the smallest letter, not the least stroke of a pen" would disappear until everything was accomplished (Matt. 5:18).

The law the disciples had known was not the law of God. It was a first-century code of religious practices designed to impress others. This form of codified behavior was harsh and oppressive. Jesus referred to it as *the righteousness of the Pharisees and the teachers of the law* (5:20). Religions based on rules and works not only have survived but also have grown because human nature prefers certainty over faith and trust.

Sometimes those who first accept Jesus Christ as Savior believe that discipleship consists of a certain code of religious practices that consists of not doing certain things. They may try to live the life of faith by religious works. It doesn't take very long for this life lived by stringent religious rules or laws to become oppressive and impossible. No amount of the things we *do not do* add up to being a Christian.

Jesus came to show that God's will goes beyond the Mosaic law. God's will is positive, based on what I *will* do rather than what I *won't* do. Jesus came to "fulfill" the law by showing that one cannot keep the law by trying to keep the law but by being the kind of person whose lifestyle flows from deeds of goodness reflecting the law's intent. The law is "fulfilled" in the *spirit* of obedience rather than in the *letter* of obedience. Paul reminds every believer that the new covenant in Jesus Christ is not expressed by the letter but by the Spirit, "for the letter kills, but the Spirit gives life." (2 Corinthians 3:6)

The disciple of Jesus Christ recognizes the necessity of the law but is guided by the impulses of the heart. The fulfillment of the law is impossible for the believer unless the Spirit within inspires and guides. God's will as interpreted by Jesus goes beyond the Mosaic law.

God's Will Demands a Higher Righteousness

John reminds us that "the law was given through Moses; grace and truth came through Jesus Christ" (John 1:17). As Jesus continued with this sermon, he clarified God's will for the Mosaic law by pointing out the truth of the higher righteousness.

Prior to the coming of Jesus to the earth, the Mosaic law consisted largely of prohibitions, such as *thou shalt not.* Jesus came to give the law a more positive meaning and practice. He changed the emphasis from what a disciple is not to do to what a disciple is to be. The disciple of Jesus is challenged to go beyond the Mosaic law, not because he has to but because he wants to. Jesus said, "For I tell you that unless your righteousness surpasses that of the Pharisees and the teachers of the law, you will certainly not enter the kingdom of heaven" (Matt. 5:20). The parables of Jesus, which spoke of God's judgment, were against a failure of duty rather than the violation of some definite law. This failure of duty represented a higher righteousness than that of the scribes and Pharisees. Jesus pointed out this higher righteousness through six illustrations:

1. *Anger (5:21–26).* The Mosaic law says "Do not murder." The will of God in the higher righteousness goes beyond the law and says, *Do not be angry and treat others with contempt.* The anger that violates the higher righteousness has its root in the human heart. It leads one to degrade another of God's creation by labeling him or her a fool. Anger is a natural emotion, but it must be managed properly without becoming destructive to oneself or others.

2. *Adultery (5:27–30).* The Mosaic law prohibited a married person's having sexual intercourse with someone other than his or her spouse. Jesus went beyond the law by teaching that looking upon a woman for the purpose of lusting for her is committing adultery with her in the heart. When the heart is ready, the action will occur if the occasion is right. Being tempted is not wrong. The writer of Hebrews reminds us that Jesus was "tempted in every way, just

as we are—yet was without sin" (Hebrews 4:15). It is *looking with the purpose of having sex*, the inner thought, that is considered adulterous.

3. *Divorce (5:31–32).* The Mosaic law permitted divorce for marital unfaithfulness. The divorce had to be accompanied by a certificate of divorce. But Jesus went beyond the mere technicalities of divorce according to Mosaic law. He dealt with the practical realities of divorce's damage done to a woman. The higher righteousness looks beyond technicalities to personal, spiritual, and emotional realities.

4. *Oaths (5:33–37).* The Mosaic law forbade a person from invoking God's name or some other sacred thing to enforce his or her testimony. Jesus went to the heart of why people swear with an oath. Swearing an oath is a method for getting one's way. It is high-handed manipulation and violates the simplicity and purity of the higher law of righteousness. A simple *yes* or *no* is good enough for the disciple.

5. *Going beyond (5:38–42).* The Mosaic law allowed retaliation for wrongdoing. Jesus taught his disciples to go beyond the Mosaic law by returning good for evil, doing more than one must to help others, and giving to people who ask.

6. *Love for enemies (5:42–48).* The final contrast between the Mosaic law and the higher righteousness is focused on what to do with our enemies. It was said that one should "love your neighbor and hate your enemy." Jesus contrasted that ethic with the higher righteousness by teaching that disciples should love their enemies even to the point of praying for them.

The higher righteousness is a way of living inspired and guided by God's goodness within the heart of the disciple.

God's Will Is Fulfilled in Spiritual Perfection

Jesus ended this section of the sermon with what appears to be an impossible command, "Be perfect, therefore, as your heavenly Father is perfect" (5:48). If Jesus was commanding his disciples to do everything as perfectly as God did, he was asking for the impossible. The Scriptures remind us, "There is no one righteous, not even one" (Romans 3:10). The Scriptures also teach that our righteousness is as filthy rags (Isaiah 64:6). How then can a disciple measure up to the perfection Jesus commands?

The perfection Jesus is commanding is found in the perfect love of God. Jesus was asked, "Teacher, which is the greatest commandment in the Law?" His response was, "Love the Lord your God with all your heart and with all your soul and with all your mind. This is the first and greatest commandment. And the second is like it: Love your neighbor as yourself. All the Law and the Prophets hang on these two commandments" (Matthew 22:37–40). The perfection Jesus is teaching is a perfection of our heart's desires, centered in the love of God.

Jesus moved beyond the law to the higher righteousness of God. It is through a life of loving deeds springing from a heart connected to a loving God that one becomes perfect as God is perfect. The only way to reach the spiritual perfection of God is to have the perfect nature of God within. Having that perfect nature provides us with the possibility of spiritual perfection. Jesus reminds us, "What is impossible with men is possible with God" (Luke 18:27).

Implications and Actions

A life of discipleship is measured by the complete goodness springing from a heart grounded in the character of God. The Mosaic law as

"RACA"

Jesus said, "Anyone who says to his brother, 'Raca,' is answerable to the Sanhedrin" (Matt. 5:22). What does the word *raca* mean, and why was a person who said it to another answerable to the Sanhedrin? The Aramaic word *raca* was a contemporary word in Jesus' day, used to make fun of someone or to exclude them. The attempt was to show contempt for a person, thus marginalizing them. When the person was marginalized, the person was fair game for worse treatment. A person who used the word *raca* of an associate could be hauled before the highest religious authority in the land, the Sanhedrin, for serious penalties.

APPLYING JESUS' TEACHINGS

To apply the teachings of Jesus in your daily walk:

- Read the Ten Commandments (Exodus 20:2–17; Deuteronomy 5:6–21), and compare them to the teachings of Jesus
- Note the people who make you angry, and list why
- Guard your mind from impure thoughts regarding sex
- Do more than you are asked to do to help someone
- Journal the name or names of your enemy or enemies, and pray for them for one week

practiced by the Pharisees and scribes magnified their goodness from the outside. Jesus taught that his disciples should cultivate the inner life, and the higher righteousness would flow supernaturally.

QUESTIONS

1. Why did Jesus begin his earthly ministry by addressing the law and the prophets?

2. What led the Pharisees to base their righteousness on the law?

3. Why is it necessary to reconcile with someone before giving an offering?

4. What makes divorce permissible?

FOCAL TEXT
Matthew 6:1–18

BACKGROUND
Matthew 6:1–18

MAIN IDEA
Jesus calls for the kind of religious practices that seek God and God's way rather than human applause and approval.

QUESTION TO EXPLORE
What's so bad about calling attention to one's religious acts?

STUDY AIM
To evaluate how I practice my faith publicly

QUICK READ
Jesus warned his disciples through three illustrations about calling attention to their own religious acts rather than seeking God's way. A mature disciple of Jesus should not do religious acts for human applause or approval.

LESSON SIX
Show Your Faith This Way—Not That Way

Collegiate and professional football officials have passed rules penalizing a team for excessive celebrations following a spectacular play, a score, or a victory. This was done so a player or team would not publicly humiliate another player or team by drawing excessive attention. One coach reminded his players against these excessive celebrations with the statement, "Act like you've been there before." He was making the point that mature players know how to give credit to others rather than taking it all for themselves.

How many believers fall into the temptation to do their religious acts "to be seen by men" (Matthew 6:1)? When Jesus used the phrase "to be seen," he used a Greek word, *theathenai*, from which we get the English word *theatrical*. Genuine disciples of Jesus Christ are not approved by God for being *theatrical* in their faith but by being genuine and humble, seeking God's way rather than human applause and approval.

MATTHEW 6:1–18

¹ Be careful not to do your 'acts of righteousness' before men, to be seen by them. If you do, you will have no reward from your Father in heaven.

² "So when you give to the needy, do not announce it with trumpets, as the hypocrites do in the synagogues and on the streets, to be honored by men. I tell you the truth, they have received their reward in full. ³ But when you give to the needy, do not let your left hand know what your right hand is doing, ⁴ so that your giving may be in secret. Then your Father, who sees what is done in secret, will reward you.

⁵ "And when you pray, do not be like the hypocrites, for they love to pray standing in the synagogues and on the street corners to be seen by men. I tell you the truth, they have received their reward in full. ⁶ But when you pray, go into your room, close the door and pray to your Father, who is unseen. Then your Father, who sees what is done in secret, will reward you. ⁷ And when you pray, do not keep on babbling like pagans, for they think they will be heard because of their many words. ⁸ Do not be like them, for your Father knows what you need before you ask him.

⁹ "This, then, is how you should pray:
"'Our Father in heaven,
      hallowed be your name,
¹⁰ your kingdom come,
your will be done
      on earth as it is in heaven.
¹¹ Give us today our daily bread.
¹² Forgive us our debts,
      as we also have forgiven our debtors.
¹³ And lead us not into temptation,
      but deliver us from the evil one.'
¹⁴ For if you forgive men when they sin against you, your heavenly Father will also forgive you. ¹⁵ But if you do not forgive men their sins, your Father will not forgive your sins.
¹⁶ "When you fast, do not look somber as the hypocrites do, for they disfigure their faces to show men they are fasting. I tell you the truth, they have received their reward in full. ¹⁷ But when you fast, put oil on your head and wash your face, ¹⁸ so that it will not be obvious to men that you are fasting, but only to your Father, who is unseen; and your Father, who sees what is done in secret, will reward you.

Buying People's Applause

Just as Jesus stated a general teaching in Matthew 5:17–20 illustrated by six antitheses in 5:21–48, so Matthew 6:1 states a general teaching illustrated by three religious practices in 6:2–18.

While disciples are encouraged to do good works before other people so *God* will be praised (Matt. 5:16), they are discouraged from doing good works so that *they* will be praised (6:1).

Jesus pointed out that the first religious practice or "act of righteousness" was giving to the needy. Giving to the needy was one of three foundational religious acts of the faithful Jew. In fact, giving, praying, and fasting were the foundations on which the good life of the Jew was based. In each of these acts Jesus was concerned with the motive for the act. As T.S. Eliot wrote, "The last temptation is the greatest treason: To do the right deed for the wrong reason."[1]

Jesus taught that giving to the needy was not to be done so others could honor you. He used the statement, "do not announce it with trumpets" (6:2). To paraphrase, *do not toot your own horn.* Some—"hypocrites," Jesus said—would put their offering money in the boxes in the women's court of the temple with such force that the clanging sounded like a trumpet. If people gave with the purpose of getting the attention and praise of others, Jesus said they had "received their reward in full" (6:2). They would not get God's attention or God's reward. As one commentator described it, "The ego is bloated and the soul shrivels."[2] One is not to give with the motive of getting a reward, but the reward comes when one gives with the right motive.

Jesus called these kinds of givers "hypocrites." Only Jesus in the New Testament used the word "hypocrite." This word is a compound word in Greek: *hupokrites,* the word for *actor.* It meant *behind the mask.* The word is taken from classical Greek where an actor on stage would hold a mask in front of the face, portraying a character. The word came to mean one who practices deceit or who impersonates another. Jesus used this word to illustrate that God wanted the face one presented to the world and the face one presented to God to be the same.

Jesus added, "Do not let your left hand know what your right hand is doing," which emphasizes the natural flow of goodness that proceeds from one's relationship to God (6:3). Giving is such a natural part of the Christian character that one does not have to think about what either

FORGIVING OTHERS

Jesus stated plainly, "If you do not forgive men their sins, your Father will not forgive your sins" (Matt. 6:15). Human forgiveness and divine forgiveness are inextricably connected. Our forgiveness of others and God's forgiveness of us cannot be separated. If we pray the model prayer while harboring an unforgiving spirit before another, we are asking God not to forgive us. We should pray the model prayer for those who have sinned against us with the same spirit of understanding and love that God has for us when we have sinned against him.

hand is doing. It is the kind of giving praised at the last judgment, "Then the righteous will answer him, 'Lord, when did we see you hungry and feed you, or thirsty and give you something to drink?'" (25:37). This kind of giving gets God's attention and reward.

The Christian motive for giving should be a heart overflowing with love for God. Paul wrote in 1 Corinthians 13:3, "If I give all I possess to the poor and surrender my body to the flames, but have not love, I gain nothing."

When a disciple gives from a heart of love, his or her giving is blessed and multiplied by God. This kind of giving is rewarded by God as God extends our spiritual influence and strengthens our faith.

Praying to the Gallery

As Jesus began his teaching on genuine prayer, he noted that the hypocrite loves to stand in the synagogue or on the street corner, praying "to be seen by men." It is obvious that this is a kind of public prayer, one of the most abused types of prayer. When one is put on the spot to pray in front of others, the pressure to perform can crowd out the need to be personal and genuine. The audience often becomes those gathered around rather than God.

Young converts who are asked to pray publicly are faced with the pressure to *measure up* to others. The need to perform and be approved by those listening is a constant worry. Spiritual maturity is sometimes judged by what one says in prayer and how one says it.

Years ago a pulpit committee visited with me about becoming pastor of their church. During the first conversation with them, one of the pulpit committee members said, "I would like to hear you pray." I was stunned by this request for a performance prayer. This request was exactly what Jesus was warning of in his teaching on prayer. Why should I pray to be heard by this man? What was his motive in hearing a prayer on demand? Was he going to judge my spiritual maturity or my theological beliefs? I politely refused the request and the opportunity to become part of that church.

Jesus told his disciples that when they prayed they should go into the closet. When Jesus said one should go into a closet to pray, he was emphasizing the need to be with God or to be alone with God so the prayer would be genuine. One can pray publicly and yet be alone with God when the prayer is genuinely prayed to God for oneself or others.

At times, Jesus went away to pray. Matthew 4 records that Jesus went into the wilderness to pray. Again, Matthew 26:36 records that Jesus went away from his disciples in the Garden of Gethsemane to pray. Jesus set the example of going into his closet to pray. Such prayer is not a prayer to impress people but to express one's deepest thoughts to God.

Pharisaical religion required a certain number of daily prayers. When a certain time came and the person was in the city, the person offered a long prayer. Jesus condemned this practice of trying to overwhelm God and impress people with many words, or "babbling." Prayer is not judged by its quantity but by its quality. We do not need to overpower God by informing God in bombastic terms about our needs. Jesus said, ". . . Your Father knows what you need before you ask him" (Matt. 6:8). God is love and is more ready to answer than we are to pray. Prayer is not getting things from God but getting into communion with God.

Jesus concluded this teaching on prayer with an example of authentic prayer, sometimes called the model prayer (6:9–13). Note that Jesus said, "This is how you should pray," not *This is what you should pray.* Jesus was not instructing the disciple that this prayer should be prayed verbatim every time prayer was offered. It should also be noted that each one of the petitions of this model prayer reflects an emphasis on

APPLYING THE PARABLE

- List three of your motives for giving financial gifts through your church
- If you offer prayer in public, consider how you can follow Jesus' standards for public prayer
- Write down the types of requests you make of God in a week of private prayers
- Pray prayers of forgiveness for someone who has sinned against you
- Try fasting before a crucial decision

the relationship of the disciple to the Father rather than on a theatrical, show-off activity. We see this in the words: "Our Father . . . your name . . . your kingdom . . . your will . . . our daily bread . . . our debts . . . our debtors." Prayer is genuine and heartfelt conversation with a loving God.

Fasting for Attention

Fasting, abstaining from food or water, should be done to focus one's energies on God and God's will. Fasting was a religious custom of the Jews in the first century, and Jesus took the practice for granted. In fact, Jesus' public ministry was preceded by a forty-day fast (4:2). We learn from this example by Jesus that fasting was done to focus Jesus' mind and energies on God's plan for his ministry.

Jesus taught his disciples that fasting was sometimes the best way to concentrate God's power on a difficult spiritual task. For instance, some early manuscripts of Mark's account of Jesus healing a boy inhabited by a violent spirit read, "This kind can come out only by prayer *and fasting*" (Mark 9:29, italics to indicate note *b*).

Fasting was practiced by the early Christians for various purposes. Following Paul's miraculous conversion on the road to Damascus, he fasted (Acts 9:9). Before the leaders of the first-century church set apart Paul and Barnabas for ministry, they fasted (Acts 13:2). As Paul and Barnabas were appointing elders in the early church, they fasted (Acts 14:23).

Jesus did not condemn fasting. He simply said that one should not try to draw attention to oneself while fasting. Jesus remarked that the hypocrites "disfigure their faces to show men they are fasting" (Matt. 6:6). The Greek word translated *disfigure* is *aphanizousi*—meaning *to make their faces disappear*. Those standing by would see them with ashes all over their faces and remark, *There goes a godly person*. Jesus said their reward would be the attention they got from others. It is what they wanted, and it is what they got. Drawing attention to oneself was drawing attention away from God.

Jesus condemned the manner of fasting that bred spiritual pride and hypocrisy. A lowly spirit did not need to be reflected in a long face. In fact, Jesus encouraged fasting accompanied by a bright and joyful face.

Instead of appearing to people that one was fasting, the person should appear that he or she was headed to a party.

Is fasting a religious activity required of a disciple today? Jesus did not demand that one fast in order to be a disciple. But Jesus did set an example showing how fasting is used of God in one's life. We also see from the example of the early church that fasting was a powerful spiritual practice used to focus their energies on important tasks.

Implications and Actions

There is a difference between doing one's religious acts publicly to be seen of other people and doing one's religious acts publicly so God will get the credit and be praised. Jesus pointed this out in Matthew 5:14–16. There is a difference between shining one's light before other people and shining one's light in other people's eyes. A disciple should give, pray, and fast for the glory of God rather than the praise of other people. It is the pleasure of God that one is seeking, not the approval of others. God sees and rewards every spiritual activity done according to God's will.

QUESTIONS

1. Why do people want credit for giving financial gifts?

2. How do public prayers differ from private prayers?

3. Why should we make requests from God when God already knows what we need before we ask?

4. How can we appear to be joyful Christians without appearing to be flippant about our faith?

NOTES ───

1. T.S. Eliot, *Murder in the Cathedral* (New York: Harcourt Brace, 1935), 44.

2. Dallas Willard, *The Divine Conspiracy: Rediscovering Our Hidden Life in God* (San Francisco: HarperSanFrancisco, 1998), 191.

MAIN IDEA
Disciples are to trust
God and value God's way
so much that they stop
emphasizing and worrying
about material things.

QUESTION TO EXPLORE
Which has our closest
attention—God or
material things?

STUDY AIM
To decide how I will focus
my life on God rather
than on material things

QUICK READ
Jesus taught that trusting God
and valuing God's way puts the
right perspective on material
things and releases one from
worrying about tomorrow's
provision. The kingdom of
God and his righteousness
should be a disciple's priority.

LESSON SEVEN
Trust God and Stop Worrying About Things

Our society teaches that things come first and God's kingdom far behind. When things come first, though, worry is a constant companion. Worry is like a rocking chair. It will give you something to do but will get you nowhere. When God's kingdom comes first, faith is a constant companion that crowds worry out of our minds.

In this section of the Sermon on the Mount, Jesus was teaching about money and its ability to take the place of God in the disciple's life. He was telling his listeners, most of whom were poor, that their security could not be found in money or possessions. Some of them probably thought, *Where then are we supposed to find our security?* That question confronts almost everyone on earth. Where does one find his or her security?

For the disciple of Jesus, security is found in serving God and seeking his kingdom and righteousness. In this teaching, Jesus is reversing the value system and security system of our world. He is saying that God's kingdom should come first, and things will naturally follow as God's provision. The challenge for the twenty-first century disciple is how to focus one's life on God while surrounded by materialistic consumerism.

MATTHEW 6:19–34

19 "Do not store up for yourselves treasures on earth, where moth and rust destroy, and where thieves break in and steal. 20 But store up for yourselves treasures in heaven, where moth and rust do not destroy, and where thieves do not break in and steal. 21 For where your treasure is, there your heart will be also.

22 "The eye is the lamp of the body. If your eyes are good, your whole body will be full of light. 23 But if your eyes are bad, your whole body will be full of darkness. If then the light within you is darkness, how great is that darkness!

24 "No one can serve two masters. Either he will hate the one and love the other, or he will be devoted to the one and despise the other. You cannot serve both God and Money.

25 "Therefore I tell you, do not worry about your life, what you will eat or drink; or about your body, what you will wear. Is not life more important than food, and the body more important than clothes? 26 Look at the birds of the air; they do not sow or reap or

store away in barns, and yet your heavenly Father feeds them. Are you not much more valuable than they? [27] Who of you by worrying can add a single hour to his life?

[28] "And why do you worry about clothes? See how the lilies of the field grow. They do not labor or spin. [29] Yet I tell you that not even Solomon in all his splendor was dressed like one of these. [30] If that is how God clothes the grass of the field, which is here today and tomorrow is thrown into the fire, will he not much more clothe you, O you of little faith? [31] So do not worry, saying, 'What shall we eat?' or 'What shall we drink?' or 'What shall we wear?' [32] For the pagans run after all these things, and your heavenly Father knows that you need them. [33] But seek first his kingdom and his righteousness, and all these things will be given to you as well. [34] Therefore do not worry about tomorrow, for tomorrow will worry about itself. Each day has enough trouble of its own.

To Serve or to Be Served (6:19–24)

Jesus challenged his disciples to consider whether they had their treasures or their treasures had them. When a person has treasures, the person can use them in God's kingdom and for God's purposes. But when treasures have a person, the person is used by his or her treasures. The writer of Proverbs illustrated with several contrasts: "He who is generous will be blessed, for he gives some of his food to the poor" (Proverbs 22:9, NASB); "A man with an evil eye hastens after wealth, and does not know that want will come upon him" (Prov. 28:22, NASB).

Jesus illustrated this contrast by referring to the eye. The eye is the part of the body that acts as a lamp by which a person sees. The treasures the earth offers are designed to capture the eye and lure the affection of the person. Recognizing the true treasure depends on the spiritual quality of the eye. The eye that is "good" (Matt. 6:22) focuses on "his kingdom and his righteousness" (6:33). When this becomes the true treasure, the disciple's entire body will be full of light. But the eye that is "bad"—wicked or godless (*poneros*, meaning *evil*)—places things before God. The evil eye fills the body with darkness, deceiving the disciple about the place of things in his or her life. Things are treasured first, before God's kingdom and righteousness.

It is clear from the teaching of Jesus that a disciple cannot serve "two masters" (6:24). A disciple either will try to live a life serving his or her possessions or will live a life serving God with his or her possessions. A disciple cannot do both.

Jesus spoke of children as a priority in the kingdom of God, saying, "Let the little children come to me, and do not hinder them, for the kingdom of heaven belongs to such as these" (19:14). Poor nutrition plays a role in at least half of the 10.9 million child deaths each year—5 million children.[1] Knowing the plight of little children around the world and hearing the words of Jesus should make all disciples examine their spending lifestyle in order to serve God with their possessions. It will mean differentiating between necessities and luxuries. Neglecting the poor speaks volumes about our treasure and our hearts.

To Worry or to Trust (6:25–32)

Jesus used the word "therefore" to introduce the next part of the sermon (Matt. 6:25). One wise seminary professor said that when one sees the word "therefore," he or she needs to ask what it is *there for.* Jesus used the word "therefore" to emphasize that one shouldn't be worried about

---

WORRY

Jesus did not suggest that a disciple should not worry—he commanded it! The English word *worry* comes from a Greek word, *merimnate,* that means to be *double-minded, to be torn in the mind, to be unstable,* or *to be anxious.* This one Greek word can translate into a complete English sentence. *Merimnate* can be translated *stop worrying,* which implies that Jesus knew his disciples were already worrying about these things. Jesus used this word in Luke 21:34, "Be careful, or your hearts will be weighed down with dissipation, drunkenness, and the anxieties of life, and that day will close on you unexpectedly like a trap." Worry is a mental anxiety that can strangle one's faith in God.

having enough earthly provisions. Worry about earthly and bodily needs can easily turn the heart away from God. Worry produces a self-fulfilling prophecy. The more we worry the less likely we are to see God's hand at work and to experience God's blessing.

Jesus taught that we can lose our sense of value when we worry about things. One person noted that worry is *irreverent* because it disobeys a direct command of Jesus, "Do not worry" (6:25). Worry is *irrelevant* because it cannot add one hour to one's life. Worry is *irresponsible* because "each day has enough trouble of its own" (6:34). Worry burns up mental and emotional energy with only negative results. Big worry equals little faith (6:30).

Disciples do not have to run after these things like the unbelievers do. All they have to do is ask God who responds the way a loving parent would respond (7:7–11).

When Jesus taught the parable of the sower and the seeds, he said, "The one who received the seed that fell among the thorns is the man who hears the word, but the worries of this life and the deceitfulness of wealth choke it, making it unfruitful" (13:22). "The deceitfulness of wealth" can destroy one's life. Human experience validates Jesus' teaching in Matthew 19:16–30 about how hard it is for a rich person to enter the kingdom of heaven.

To Seek First or to Seek Last (6:33–34)

Jesus ended this part of the sermon by emphasizing the priority of the disciple's life—"his kingdom and his righteousness." Jesus lumped together "his kingdom and his righteousness" with "these things" by putting them in their proper order. "Pagans run after" things, making things their priority. The disciple is supposed to run after the kingdom and righteousness and wait on God to provide "these things."

A tour guide made an interesting observation about a group of Americans touring famous places. When the buses drove up to the museums, at least one-third of the visitors on being discharged from a tour bus entered the museum foyer first and looked around for the museum shop. They then purchased some object in the museum shop, represented and labeled by the museum as one of its best known objects. The tourists then returned to the bus without ever entering the museum galleries. The tour guide observed that such is the superficiality of Americans today— they want the souvenirs without the experience.

Jesus warned about those who go through life wanting life's souvenirs without having an experience with the Giver of life. A disciple is to seek first God and his kingdom; the souvenirs will be added later.

We should live each day with the faith that God knows our needs and will provide what we need. God may not provide all we want in terms of prosperity and affluence, but God promises to provide "all these things" (6:33) necessary for survival and life.

It is often difficult to reconcile this teaching on God's provision when we see the great disparity in "things" between America and much of the rest of the world. How does God intend to provide for believers in poverty-stricken circumstances? He made it clear in Matthew 25:31–46 that a person "blessed by my Father," a person who has experienced God's blessing of eternal life, will be a channel for God's provision of "these things." Less fortunate people are fed and clothed through disciples who understand how to put God's kingdom and righteousness first. God blesses believers that they might be a blessing to others.

Among the couples in my experience who have most personified kingdom priorities with their material goods were two physicians. They were members of the church where I was pastor. Although they made more money than most of the church members, they lived in a modest home, drove older automobiles, and wore their clothes for years. The couple consistently housed exchange students, worked on a mercy ship, and gave aid to the poor in our city. They could have lived in the highest

APPLYING THE SERMON

- Make an inventory of your most valuable possessions
- Write down the reasons you purchased these possessions
- Reflect on your basic need for these possessions
- Compare the value of these possessions to some of the basic needs of the poor in your community
- Commit to adding a spiritual dimension to your spending lifestyle

society with the costliest of things, but they chose to live a modest life-style so they could put God's kingdom and righteousness first.

It is unfortunate that some people involuntarily put God's kingdom and righteousness last by virtue of being trapped in a money-focused lifestyle. Through the use of easy credit or simply through ignoring the needs of others to get stuff they really don't need, they put God's kingdom and righteousness last.

Putting God's kingdom and righteousness first means we will not wear ourselves out in the unnecessary race to accumulate things. Neither will we worry ourselves into an early grave.

Applying the Lesson to Life

Balancing the priority of God's kingdom and his righteousness with the abundance of things is a challenging spiritual task. Paul reminds us in Romans 14:17, "For the kingdom of God is not a matter of eating and drinking, but of righteousness, peace and joy in the Holy Spirit."

Paul also reminds us in Romans 1:17, "For in the gospel a righteous-ness from God is revealed, a righteousness that is by faith from first to last, just as it is written: 'The righteous will live by faith.'" Putting God's kingdom and righteousness first and not worrying about things is a walk of faith from first to last.

The disciple must believe Jesus' words more than he or she believes the words of any other person. The disciple of Jesus must shape a lifestyle based on this belief rather than on any prevailing custom or religious teaching. The disciple should remember that today is the tomorrow he or she worried about yesterday.

QUESTIONS

1. How does one store up treasures in heaven?

2. How does one keep his or her spiritual eyes good?

3. What two major worries keep you from trusting God for his
    provision?

4. How do you express *big* faith as opposed to *little* faith?

5. How can your treasures serve God's kingdom and righteousness?

NOTES

1. http://www.worldhunger.org/articles/Learn/child_hunger_facts.htm. Accessed 7/15/11.

FOCAL TEXT
Matthew 7:1–27

BACKGROUND
Matthew 7:1–29

MAIN IDEA
Truly living as Jesus' disciple demands deliberately choosing to follow Jesus' teachings in relating to other people and to God.

QUESTION TO EXPLORE
What difference would following Jesus' teachings make in how you relate to other people and to God?

STUDY AIM
To identify ways I will put Jesus' teachings into practice as his disciple

QUICK READ
Being Jesus' disciple calls for obedience to Jesus' teachings rather than mere intellectual assent to these teachings.

LESSON EIGHT
Make the Right Choice

One Sunday afternoon while returning from morning worship, my wife and I turned into our new neighborhood and noticed a neighbor mowing his lawn with a riding lawnmower. As we approached this neighbor, I launched into a criticism about how lazy some people are to ride a lawn-mower on a small postage stamp-sized lawn. I added something to the effect that this is what is wrong with our country today.

As we got closer, we could see that the man riding the mower didn't have legs. It became very quiet in the car until my wife commented, "And you were saying. . . ?" It didn't take a spiritual giant to tell me I had disobeyed the teachings of Jesus on judging others. I could have saved myself a lot of mental and spiritual pain if I had treated this neighbor the way I would have wanted him to treat me.

MATTHEW 7:1–27

¹ "Do not judge, or you too will be judged. ² For in the same way you judge others, you will be judged, and with the measure you use, it will be measured to you.

³ "Why do you look at the speck of sawdust in your brother's eye and pay no attention to the plank in your own eye? ⁴ How can you say to your brother, 'Let me take the speck out of your eye,' when all the time there is a plank in your own eye? ⁵ You hypocrite, first take the plank out of your own eye, and then you will see clearly to remove the speck from your brother's eye.

⁶ "Do not give dogs what is sacred; do not throw your pearls to pigs. If you do, they may trample them under their feet, and then turn and tear you to pieces.

⁷ "Ask and it will be given to you; seek and you will find; knock and the door will be opened to you. ⁸ For everyone who asks receives; he who seeks finds; and to him who knocks, the door will be opened.

⁹ "Which of you, if his son asks for bread, will give him a stone? ¹⁰ Or if he asks for a fish, will give him a snake? ¹¹ If you, then, though you are evil, know how to give good gifts to your children, how much more will your Father in heaven give good gifts to those who ask him! ¹² So in everything, do to others what you would have them do to you, for this sums up the Law and the Prophets.

[13] "Enter through the narrow gate. For wide is the gate and broad is the road that leads to destruction, and many enter through it. [14] But small is the gate and narrow the road that leads to life, and only a few find it.

[15] "Watch out for false prophets. They come to you in sheep's clothing, but inwardly they are ferocious wolves. [16] By their fruit you will recognize them. Do people pick grapes from thornbushes, or figs from thistles? [17] Likewise every good tree bears good fruit, but a bad tree bears bad fruit. [18] A good tree cannot bear bad fruit, and a bad tree cannot bear good fruit. [19] Every tree that does not bear good fruit is cut down and thrown into the fire. [20] Thus, by their fruit you will recognize them.

[21] "Not everyone who says to me, 'Lord, Lord,' will enter the kingdom of heaven, but only he who does the will of my Father who is in heaven. [22] Many will say to me on that day, 'Lord, Lord, did we not prophesy in your name, and in your name drive out demons and perform many miracles?' [23] Then I will tell them plainly, 'I never knew you. Away from me, you evildoers!'

[24] "Therefore everyone who hears these words of mine and puts them into practice is like a wise man who built his house on the rock. [25] The rain came down, the streams rose, and the winds blew and beat against that house; yet it did not fall, because it had its foundation on the rock. [26] But everyone who hears these words of mine and does not put them into practice is like a foolish man who built his house on sand. [27] The rain came down, the streams rose, and the winds blew and beat against that house, and it fell with a great crash."

Relating to Others Through Criticism or Understanding (7:1–6)

The first six verses of Matthew 7 deal with the unspiritual way disciples try to control those around them by blaming or condemning them. Unfortunately some believers have greater confidence in the power of condemnation or criticism to straighten others out than they do in what's been called the *Golden Rule*: "So in everything, do to others what you would have them do to you" (Matthew 7:12).

Jesus' command in verse 1, "Do not judge," is clarified in verse 16a, "By their fruit you will recognize them." It is natural for one to recognize or distinguish "fruit" (good behavior from bad). But it is wrong to "judge" the behavior because one may not have all the facts behind the behavior. Only the Holy Spirit can "judge" the reasons for a person's behavior. It is often more comfortable to talk about the mistakes in another's life than to face up to the sins in our own life.

A disciple's attention and focus should first be given to his or her own behavior before trying to render a verdict on another's behavior. Jesus likened the behavior of the one judging to someone with a board in his own eye trying to discern a speck in another's eye, or having a plank in his own eye and trying to discern a splinter in another's eye. Condemnation or criticism is the board in the eye of the judge. Condemnation blinds us to the reality of the other person. We have difficulty seeing how to help the other person because we cannot see the other person. We can only see our censorious perspective. A disciple of Jesus Christ should never go around *fault-finding and flaw-picking.*

Being a *fruit inspector* (Matt. 7:16) rather than a judge is the proper perspective of a disciple of Jesus. We should form an opinion about what we see rather than give a verdict about what we think about what we see. We can observe another's actions without judging the person's motives. This distinction can sometimes be difficult for the new believer whose conversion has come with a zeal for the study of the Scriptures. The new

WOLVES IN SHEEP'S CLOTHING

A *wolf in sheep's clothing* is one who is living a life of deception. Outwardly the person looks like a sheep but inwardly the person is thinking about devouring the sheep. The person looks good but inwardly is governed by his or her own desires. This is a description of a religious person who is trying to use others for his or her own purposes. Jude spoke of these in Jude 12a and 16, "These men are blemishes at your love feasts, eating with you without the slightest qualm—shepherds who feed only themselves. . . ; These men are grumblers and faultfinders; they follow their own evil desires; they boast about themselves and flatter others for their own advantage."

believer may be relating to people based on doctrinal correctness rather than the grace of God. As has been said, "There is so much good in the worst of us, and so much bad in the best of us, that it hardly behooves any of us to talk about the rest of us."[1]

When Jesus warns about throwing sacred things or pearls to dogs or pigs, he is not degrading other people. He is teaching us that we cannot force spiritual practices on those who do not want them or cannot understand them. A dog cannot digest a sacred thing, and neither can a pig digest a pearl. These valuable things would be worthless to them. The same is true of our efforts to force precious spiritual teachings on someone to whom they make no sense. We have the solution they need without their knowing they have a problem. Forcing these issues can become our way of trying to control the other person. We judge them. We know what's best for them more than they know what's best for them. This kind of heavy-handed religion can make the person "turn and tear you to pieces" (7:6).

Relating to God by Asking, Seeking, and Knocking (7:7–11)

Jesus used the illustration of a good father providing for his children to point out the nature of a loving God. If flawed parents know how to give good gifts to their children, how much more does God know how to give good gifts to those who ask him. The "good gifts" are those gifts that belong to the kingdom of God. They are listed in the Model Prayer in Matthew 6, as daily bread, daily forgiveness, daily protection from temptation, and daily protection from the evil one.

Prayer relates to God and others. We pray to God that we might relate in the proper spiritual way to others. Prayer prepares our hearts for obedience to the teachings of Jesus. In order to treat others as we would have them treat us, we have to be on speaking terms with God. We know from verses 1–5 that we are not to judge others but to discern our own spiritual condition. After we have discerned our own spiritual condition, then we can turn to a loving Father to ask for him to supply what we lack.

When Jesus said a disciple should *ask, seek,* and *knock,* the original Greek words are imperatives or commands in the present tense and call for continuing action. A literal translation would be *keep on asking, keep on seeking, keep on knocking.* The use of these three verbs indicates intensity.

Asking God in prayer reinforces a humble approach to God and to others. Asking in prayer reinforces our consciousness of a personal and giving God. The asking of a disciple should be specific. Paul wrote in Philippians 4:6, "present your requests to God."

Seeking God means asking plus taking deliberate action. When Jesus told his disciples to pray, "Give us today our daily bread," he didn't mean a disciple should just pray and sit around doing nothing to get daily bread. Seeking means to ask God and then look for the opportunity to be a part of the answer. Paul was explicit about that spiritual principle in 2 Thessalonians 3:10, "If a man will not work, he shall not eat."

Knocking is asking and seeking persistently. In Luke 11:5–8, Jesus illustrated persistent prayer by telling about a man who knocked at his neighbor's door until the neighbor got up and answered. Again in Luke 18:1, Jesus told his disciples a parable to show them that they should always pray and not give up.

God will always answer our prayers in his way and for our best spiritual interest. Jesus tells us in this passage that God will answer according to the wisdom of a loving parent, "For everyone who asks receives" (Matt. 7:8a). This is a strong incentive for every disciple to understand that God makes no exceptions among his children.

A JUDGING DILEMMA

Frank Parsons taught a tenth-grade boy's Sunday School class at a Baptist church. For several weeks, one of his students, John Pierce, seemed to be carrying a big problem. One day after class, Frank asked John how he was doing. This opened the door for young John to share what was happening in his home. John's father, one of the lay leaders in the church, was constantly criticizing and condemning John when he was at home. John felt as if his father didn't really love him. He saw his father embracing others at church and encouraging them but he saw a different father at home. If you were Frank Parsons, how would you help John's father correct this judgmental and destructive spirit?

Relating to Jesus Through Obedience (7:13–27)

Jesus used four contrasts to illustrate the necessity for a disciple to be obedient to his teachings:

1. *The Narrow and Wide Gate (7:13–14).* The narrow gate does not represent more religious rules or doctrinal correctness. The narrow gate is obedience to the teachings of Jesus. When a person has faith in Jesus Christ, he or she has confidence in following Jesus' teachings. On the other hand, there are those who are rigidly correct in doctrine but have hearts as cold as stone.

    The narrow gate leads down a narrow road. Obedience is not a one-time thing but an all-time thing. Coming into the kingdom through obedience to one's confession of faith in Jesus Christ leads to one's journey in obedience to Jesus as Lord.

    Those who choose the broad road are those who do as they please without considering the teachings of Jesus. This broad road leads to a destructive lifestyle. There are many who refuse to be obedient to the teachings of Jesus and wind up on this broad road.

2. *The Good Tree and the Bad Tree (7:15–20).* When we have fellowship with Jesus Christ, we respond in obedience to him from the good within. The "good tree" produces "good fruit" from the kind of disciple one has become in relationship with Jesus. These disciples differ from the *wolves in sheep's clothing*, who put on an outward show of discipleship without an inner change. They represent the "bad tree," which "cannot bear good fruit.' Jesus said in Matthew 12:33–35, "Make a tree good and its fruit will be good, or make a tree bad and its fruit will be bad, for a tree is recognized by its fruit. You brood of vipers, how can you who are evil say anything good? For out of the overflow of the heart the mouth speaks. The good man brings good things out of the good stored up in him, and the evil man brings evil things out of the evil stored up in him."

3. *The Will of God and Great Deeds in His Name (7:21–23).* Doing great deeds in Jesus' name or calling him Lord are no substitute for being obedient to Jesus' teachings. The one who enters the kingdom of heaven is the one who actually does the will of God. Jesus responded to the criticism of the Pharisees by saying, "But

wisdom is proved right by her actions" (11:19b). It is much easier to say "Lord, Lord" than to make Jesus Lord of every activity in life. Being obedient to the teachings of Jesus may not always be as noticeable as *driving out demons and performing miracles*, but obedience is a more certain way of entering the kingdom of God.

4. *The House on the Sand and the House on the Rock (7:24–27).* The person who puts Jesus' teachings into practice as a lifestyle builds a life that is indestructible because it is built on the rock. Paul reminds us that this rock is Jesus Christ (1 Corinthians 10:4). The stable life lived on the rock is a life of spiritual strength and spiritual understanding. When one is obedient to the teachings of Jesus Christ, an inner strength flows out to bless the lives of others.

Applying the Lesson to Life

How we treat others is an indication of our faith in Jesus Christ and our obedience to his teachings. Our primary attention should be on our relationship to Jesus Christ and the authenticity with which we live out our faith. The guiding principle for our behavior toward others is found in verse 12, "So in everything, do to others what you would have them do to you, for this sums up the Law and the Prophets." When we live according to this teaching, we will produce good fruit and will build our lives on a rock solid foundation.

QUESTIONS

1. Why is the spirit of judgment prevalent among Christians?

2. How does one give that which is sacred to dogs or throw pearls to pigs?

3. How long should one persist in a specific prayer request?

4. What makes the road leading to life narrow?

5. Why is the confession, "Lord, Lord," not adequate for salvation?

NOTES ————————————————————————————————

1. Attributed to Edward Wallis Hoch (1849–1925).

—— U N I T   T H R E E ——

Further Instructions on Genuine Discipleship

Unit three, "Further Instructions on Genuine Discipleship," provides further instructions from Jesus that clarify the true nature of discipleship. The four lessons in this unit deal with passages selected from Matthew 8—16 that speak pointedly to what being Jesus' disciple means.

UNIT THREE. FURTHER INSTRUCTIONS ON GENUINE DISCIPLESHIP

MAIN IDEA
Jesus demands that his
disciples place him over the
most legitimate and precious
of human concerns, even
shelter and family, as well
as cultural expectations.

QUESTION TO EXPLORE
How far should we go
in following Jesus?

STUDY AIM
To describe how the radical
nature of discipleship to
Jesus applies to my life

QUICK READ
Jesus taught two would-be
disciples that he must have
priority in their lives.

LESSON NINE
*Face the Radical
Nature of
Discipleship*

My wife's father died suddenly on a Monday morning some years ago. Compounding our grief was that we were considering leaving a pastorate in Atlanta, Georgia, for me to serve as pastor in Harrodsburg, Kentucky. I had preached at the Kentucky church the day before he died. As we made our way through grief and decision-making, I came home late one night. Everyone was in bed, including my wife. However, a lamp was on in our bedroom, where her open Bible revealed that she had underlined several phrases from Luke 9:57–62, a similar passage to today's text from Matthew.

The underlined section included these words, "Let me go and bury my father . . . let the dead bury their own dead . . . go and proclaim the kingdom of God" (Luke 9:59b–60). I had not been able to get past Paul's admonition to Timothy concerning taking care of your family (1 Timothy 5:8), but my wife had a bigger faith and better understanding than I had. These words of Jesus were not harsh or uncaring but a pointed reminder of the higher priority that comes with being a follower of Jesus. Our struggle was how to respond to God's will to follow him while at the same time doing God's will in caring for people we loved. God's grace enabled us to do both.

MATTHEW 8:18–22

18 When Jesus saw the crowd around him, he gave orders to cross to the other side of the lake. 19 Then a teacher of the law came to him and said, "Teacher, I will follow you wherever you go."

20 Jesus replied, "Foxes have holes and birds of the air have nests, but the Son of Man has no place to lay his head."

21 Another disciple said to him, "Lord, first let me go and bury my father."

22 But Jesus told him, "Follow me, and let the dead bury their own dead."

A Time to Get Away (8:18)

Some think of Matthew 8—9 in terms of miracles. Jesus healed a man of leprosy (Matthew 8:1–4) and a centurion's servant due to the remarkable faith of the centurion (Matt. 8:5–13). He healed many others, including Simon Peter's mother-in-law (8:14–16). Later, Jesus calmed a storm while he and his disciples were crossing the Sea of Galilee (8:23–27). When they arrived on land, Jesus healed two demon-possessed men and performed remarkable acts with demons and a herd of pigs (8:28–34). Jesus performed other miracles in chapter 9. Along with all of this, two things were happening: (1) crowds were becoming enthusiastic about Jesus; and (2) the religious leaders were growing increasingly uncomfortable with what Jesus was doing and who he claimed to be.

Jesus had left the crowds earlier in Matthew (5:1), when he directed his teaching in chapters 5—8, what we call the Sermon on the Mount, to his disciples. These chapters have been the focus of the previous five studies. When Jesus came down the mountain and was met by large crowds (8:1), Jesus again took his disciples away from the crowds. Before he could get to the boat, however, he was met by two people who professed an interest in being his disciples.

Many pastors dream of preaching before large crowds and in sanctuaries full of people. Some get to do that, and there is a place for ministering to large crowds. But, Jesus had another agenda for his disciples, and more personalized instruction was needed. These followers were foundational people for the future. Preparing people to live and serve effectively in the future is important business, then and now, whether in a large group setting or a more personalized one.

Jesus knew it was time to move away from the crowds. Some folks were curious about him, but they generally were more fascinated with the miracles he did (see John 2:24; 4:48). Before Jesus could board the boat, two people stopped him. That happened more than once in Jesus' life. Sometimes, ministry opportunities just happen, regardless of what our schedule or plans are.

Think About It! (8:19–20)

The first person to stop Jesus was a "teacher of the law," sometimes referred to as a scribe. This prominent person appeared to make the necessary commitment, "I will follow you wherever you go." Peers of this man would later become chief critics of Jesus, but at this point, this teacher was committing himself to Jesus, whom he called "teacher" (*rabbi*). He wanted to be a disciple of Jesus. Jesus did not turn down his offer or cast suspicion on his group identity, but he did make him think about his commitment.

Jesus told him that "the Son of Man has no place to lay his head." This is the first time Jesus used "Son of Man" to describe himself. A knowledgeable scribe would know the various meanings of the phrase from Old Testament and extra-biblical writings. It appears to have been Jesus' favorite way to refer to himself and was used eighty times in the Gospels. Its usage here follows Matthew's linking Jesus to the concept of the Messiah as a Suffering Servant (Matt. 8:16–17). The rich meanings of Son of Man, Suffering Servant, and Messiah are fertile ground for deeper study; Jesus' use of the phrase "Son of Man" gave the man more to think about.

Discipleship demands discipline and is costly to all who would follow Jesus. On another occasion when Jesus was teaching about the meaning of following him, Jesus said, *Count the cost* (Luke 14:28).

A REGENERATE CHURCH MEMBERSHIP

In the early days of the seventeenth century, the Anabaptists of Europe and Baptists in England both emphasized the importance of a church being composed of regenerated believers. Members were regenerated, *born again* or *born from above* (John 3:3). Church was not something one entered by a natural birth but by a spiritual rebirth. Their convictions were far deeper than protesting infant baptism. Regenerated believers were expected to live a disciplined life, following the teachings of Jesus.

Two large groups of members in many Baptist churches are non-resident members and inactive members who live in the area of the church. Also, baptismal statistics indicate that many children are baptized at a very young age. Do these trends reflect a regenerate church membership or a slippage into casual Christianity that does not emphasize discipline, spiritual growth, and fervency in our commitment to Christ? Elton Trueblood (1900–1994), Quaker author and theologian, wrote a book in which he described the church as the "company of the committed."[1] Does that describe you and your church today?

Jesus' response in Matthew 8:20 was also especially pertinent to the circumstance of a scribe or teacher. The workshop of a scribe was not in the public arena but in the calm and safety of a home while working through the scrolls. Although it was remarkable for fishermen to lay aside their boats and nets to follow Jesus, it would have been more demanding for a teacher of respected position to give up his lifestyle to join the traveling band of disciples.

Note what Jesus was not saying. He was not arguing against having a home. His mother and family lived in Nazareth, and one of the healing miracles of Matthew 8 happened in the home of Simon Peter's mother-in-law. Jesus stayed in the home of Mary, Martha, and Lazarus in Bethany. Many churches of the first century met in homes. "No place to lay his head" may be a metaphorical way of expressing what John wrote in John 1:11: "He came to that which was his own, but his own did not receive him."

People can be obsessed and filled with pride about the things of this world, including a place to lay their heads. We accommodate ourselves easily to our culture and may forget how the story of Jesus' life began in a borrowed stable and ended in a borrowed tomb. When we commit to follow Jesus, we commit ourselves to One who lived well but simply. Perhaps we all could live more modestly while using our means to help others live better.

Understand the Right Priority (8:21–22)

Jesus' pointed words in Matthew 8:21–22 do not teach one to disrespect or dishonor parents.

Later in Matthew 15:3–6, Jesus talked about the importance of honoring one's father and mother. That is one of the Ten Commandments. Jesus did not come to trash the commandments but to fill them full with meaning (Matt. 5:17).

The second person to stop Jesus is identified as "another disciple." That may mean that both of these people who stopped Jesus were disciples, or it could simply mean that this second person was in the broad group of disciples who gathered around Jesus, although not one of the twelve apostles. Regardless, he too expressed his commitment to Jesus, but he was not as impulsive or decisive, saying, "Lord, first let me go and bury my father." This disciple is an example of a person who had the wrong thing in first place in life.

Jesus knew that the man's loyalty and priority were wrong if he wanted to be Jesus' disciple. Jesus' response was two-fold: (1) follow me; and (2) let the dead bury their own dead. The first command is one of the simplest *plans of salvation* that we have. To be a disciple of Jesus, you have to *follow Jesus.* Jesus expanded in Matthew 16 what that means, which is the focus of lesson eleven. In that passage, Jesus told Peter "get behind me" (16:23). How often we want to be first in line, but Jesus says to get in line behind him. It may have been a childhood game to *follow the leader,* but it's the way of salvation to *follow the Leader,* Jesus.

The second part of Jesus' response was "let the dead bury their dead." The normal practice of the first century was to bury people on the day they died. Doing that was viewed as a sacred responsibility of the family; however, this man would not have been following Jesus if his father had died on the day he spoke to Jesus. He was not in grief but in waiting. He wanted to defer to a later date, a more convenient time. He saw enough in Jesus to follow him, but his commitment was weak. He was a follower, but he wanted to wait to make a deeper commitment until he dealt with other interests. Jesus' response had nothing to do with dishonoring parents, but he called on the man to have the right priority and stop using good-sounding excuses instead of following him.

Jesus did not think the man was spiritually dead. He saw something greater in him than the man saw in himself. The world is full of

RADICAL OR CASUAL?

You deliberately took this *Adult Bible Study Guide* to a doctor's office, intending to study this lesson while you waited. The person sitting beside you saw the title of this lesson, "Face the Radical Nature of Discipleship." Entering into conversation with you, she asked, "What is radical about discipleship?" Synonyms of "radical" include *thorough, drastic, deep-seated, major, far-reaching, extreme,* and *drastic.* How would you illustrate from your life that your faith is not casual but committed, that your faith goes beyond the *normal* to that which is explainable only as a person totally committed to Jesus Christ?

spiritually dead people, but Jesus saw something alive and promising in the man. *Let the spiritually dead take care of the spiritually dead things of the world* was Jesus' message to the man. He was also telling him, *This is your moment, follow me.* Those who follow Jesus have a different priority and a different mission.

This Lesson and Life

People, whether Christian or not, are concerned about similar basic things. Housing, family, work, volunteer opportunities, recreation, politics, and lifestyle are just a few of many concerns and options we face. Each and all can be impacted positively by a whole-hearted commitment to Jesus Christ. Likewise in each, we face a tension about how we really do life. The tension is not necessarily bad, for it keeps us aware that being a disciple of Christ is a fulltime effort.

You may have a prick of conscience when you decide to watch NCAA basketball tournament games rather than study a Bible study lesson. You may wrestle with the best ways to use money or time. Life has its choices. The focus of today's text is to understand the importance of a radical and dynamic commitment to Christ, because that is what God desires and what we truly need. That commitment then becomes the filter through which we live, in dealing with the big and small issues of life. Life is complex, but some things can be simplified once the first priority is realized. You can live a whole-hearted commitment to Christ that pleases God, strengthens others, and brings satisfaction within your soul.

QUESTIONS

1. What excuses have you heard or used to evade an opportunity to serve or honor Christ?

2. When have you acted impulsively and it was the right thing to do?

3. We sometimes read about *the cost of discipleship.* What is the cost of *not* being a follower of Jesus?

4. How can you help someone else to have a more deeply committed relationship with God?

5. If you could change one thing about yourself in your relationships with family, what would that be?

6. How would you describe your plan for spiritual growth and maturity?

NOTES ——————————————————————————————————

1. Elton Trueblood, *The Company of the Committed.* New York: Harper and Row, 1961. See http://www.ccel.us/company.toc.html. Accessed 7/18/11.

LESSON TEN

What Jesus' Disciples Do

FOCAL TEXT
Matthew 9:35—10:15, 24–31

BACKGROUND
Matthew 9:35—11:1

MAIN IDEA
Jesus calls his disciples
to engage in his mission
and provides instructions
for doing so.

QUESTION TO EXPLORE
How do Jesus' instructions
to his disciples to follow
as they participated in his
mission apply to us today?

STUDY AIM
To evaluate how I am following
Jesus' instructions as I
participate in his mission

QUICK READ
Jesus called disciples to a
whole-hearted commitment
and instructed them in how to
do his mission and ministry.

When I arrived at a high school to meet with the principal about a school matter, students were everywhere, in what initially appeared to be total chaos. Four big young men immediately stepped in front of me. Each looked like a college tackle in football. One asked, "Hey, man, what do you do?" I said, "I do a lot of things." I told them that I was pastor of a church, and another said, "Yeah, man, but what is your vocation?"

I had walked in on *vocations day* at the high school, and they assumed I was there to talk about my work. Their questions were perhaps bigger than they intended. As a Christian, I am committed to Jesus Christ as my Lord and Savior. That is my vocation, my calling in life. I have lived that in many roles, including being a pastor. Both issues the students raised are pertinent to today's Scripture: our vocation is that we are called to be disciples of Jesus Christ. He expects us to *do* mission and ministry according to his instructions, our gifts, and the opportunities and needs we see.

MATTHEW 9:35–38

[35] Jesus went through all the towns and villages, teaching in their synagogues, preaching the good news of the kingdom and healing every disease and sickness. [36] When he saw the crowds, he had compassion on them, because they were harassed and helpless, like sheep without a shepherd. [37] Then he said to his disciples, "The harvest is plentiful but the workers are few. [38] Ask the Lord of the harvest, therefore, to send out workers into his harvest field."

MATTHEW 10:1–15, 24–31

[1] He called his twelve disciples to him and gave them authority to drive out evil spirits and to heal every disease and sickness.

[2] These are the names of the twelve apostles: first, Simon (who is called Peter) and his brother Andrew; James son of Zebedee, and his brother John; [3] Philip and Bartholomew; Thomas and Matthew the tax collector; James son of Alphaeus, and Thaddaeus; [4] Simon the Zealot and Judas Iscariot, who betrayed him.

[5] These twelve Jesus sent out with the following instructions: "Do not go among the Gentiles or enter any town of the Samaritans. [6] Go rather to the lost sheep of Israel. [7] As you go, preach this message: 'The kingdom of heaven is near.' [8] Heal the sick, raise the dead, cleanse those who have leprosy, drive out demons. Freely you have received, freely give. [9] Do not take along any gold or silver or copper in your belts; [10] take no bag for the journey, or extra tunic, or sandals or a staff; for the worker is worth his keep.

[11] "Whatever town or village you enter, search for some worthy person there and stay at his house until you leave. [12] As you enter the home, give it your greeting. [13] If the home is deserving, let your peace rest on it; if it is not, let your peace return to you. [14] If anyone will not welcome you or listen to your words, shake the dust off your feet when you leave that home or town. [15] I tell you the truth, it will be more bearable for Sodom and Gomorrah on the day of judgment than for that town.

. . . .

[24] "A student is not above his teacher, nor a servant above his master. [25] It is enough for the student to be like his teacher, and the servant like his master. If the head of the house has been called Beelzebub, how much more the members of his household!

[26] "So do not be afraid of them. There is nothing concealed that will not be disclosed, or hidden that will not be made known. [27] What I tell you in the dark, speak in the daylight; what is whispered in your ear, proclaim from the roofs. [28] Do not be afraid of those who kill the body but cannot kill the soul. Rather, be afraid of the One who can destroy both soul and body in hell. [29] Are not two sparrows sold for a penny? Yet not one of them will fall to the ground apart from the will of your Father. [30] And even the very hairs of your head are all numbered. [31] So don't be afraid; you are worth more than many sparrows.

Jesus' Ministry Continues Through Disciples (9:35—10:4)

Jesus did not sit under a tree or in a pleasant sanctuary waiting for the world to come to him, but he traveled through "all the town and villages, teaching in their synagogues" (Matthew 9:35). Matthew wrote earlier about Jesus' ministry of teaching, preaching, and healing (Matt. 4:23). In this lesson's text, Matthew added to that earlier summary statement by writing about Jesus' compassion for needy people. Jesus had compassion, a heart broken by what he saw. People were harassed and helpless, confused and aimless. They needed someone to care for them and guide them. Jesus saw great potential in them, but they needed someone to extend the grace and love of God. These people did not need more rules, excessive burdens, and accusing fingers (see 23:1–37). In contrast, Jesus knew the twelve disciples could be *like* him. They could be the kind of shepherds and workers that the crowds needed.

Why did Jesus tell his disciples to pray to God for workers in the harvest? His call to pray had nothing to do with God's willingness to send workers but everything to do with the need for followers to accept the call. We must pray, but we must do more than pray. Jesus used two metaphors in these verses: shepherds and workers in the fields. The shepherd cares for and meets the needs of people. When we begin to pray, we become a worker in the harvest on behalf of the Good Shepherd (see John 10:11), for evangelism and spiritual growth. Jesus anticipated that many in the crowd would become his followers, but disciples need to be intentional about going to work in the field.

Jesus commanded them to pray for workers, and then he provided the answer to the prayer: Jesus called the twelve disciples together and gave them unusual spiritual power (Matt. 10:1). The Twelve were first chosen to be with Jesus (Mark 3:14), but their bigger purpose was unfolding. They had responded to Jesus' "follow me" into discipleship (Matt. 4:18–22; 9:9). Now they were being commissioned, instructed, and empowered for mission. The Lord promised and guaranteed the harvest (9:37; see 13:1–9, 18–23).

Consider what Jesus said of his mission just hours before his crucifixion: "For this reason I was born and for this I came into the world, to testify to the truth" (John 18:37). Although the disciples might not have realized it, being on mission without Jesus physically present was why they were called to follow him. These disciples had heard Jesus teach in the Sermon on the Mount (Matt. 5:13–16) about being salt and light. Now, they were at a pivotal moment when they would practice what they had been taught. They would take the salt and light into the world; it would not be hidden or concealed. Jesus had another command, *go*. The mission of Jesus was now theirs.

Jesus Sends Out Disciples (10:5–15)

We are familiar with laboratory experiences and test runs. Jesus did something like these with his disciples. He continued to prepare them for a time he would no longer be physically tutoring them. He sent them *out* (10:5). God still sends people out; however, he told these disciples to "go rather to the lost sheep of Israel" (10:6). You have to start somewhere; Jesus started their mission experience among the people and culture that they knew. This instruction, as well as others, had local and temporary application. Matthew closed his Gospel account with the Great Commission (28:18–20), which supersedes this command and embraces the world vision in making disciples. Paul similarly noted that the gospel was given to the Jews first and then to the Gentiles (Romans 1:16). Mission trips around the world and with different cultures are needed, but we must not forget to start where we are.

One part of the disciples' message was "the kingdom of heaven is near" (Matt. 10:7). Jesus was the earthly embodiment of all that was good and right about the kingdom. He was literally near to those who would hear the disciples. This quotation also is an affirmation of the disciples. Through their efforts, people would hear the gospel, be healed, and see miracles. All these were evidences that God was doing something wonderful in their midst and that God was using the disciples in his mission.

These instructions of Jesus are not rules for every era and for every mission of the church. Some were reversed (Luke 22:35–38); however, a consideration of what they meant to these first disciples can help us in the twenty-first century. We can still "preach the message" (Matt. 10:8), using various methods of proclamation and service. Few if any of us have the power to heal people, raise the dead, and cast out demons as these disciples did, though. Other considerations in the text fit the pattern of a short, limited trip. Although the disciples served freely, Jesus did remind us of what is later taught more completely in the New Testament, "the worker is worth his keep (10:10).

"Shake the dust off your feet" (10:14) is still good advice. The command teaches figuratively that we cannot win them all, but neither did Jesus. Not everyone will embrace the gospel; however, we do not let indifference, rejection, or our weaknesses disable us. The disciples could have wallowed in self-pity if some did not receive them or their message, but instead, they were to "shake the dust off your feet" and continue on to the next town or village. This understanding does not imply that we quit and leave town but that our responsibility is to be faithful disciples and messengers of the love and message of God. We do the best we can and leave the results to God. We don't quit on Jesus or the mission.

Jesus Challenges and Encourages (10:24–31)

The thought that we can be "like" Jesus is amazing (Matt. 10:24–25). It is a great encouragement as well as our goal; however, Jesus used that thought to teach the Twelve about the reality and cost of being a disciple. Jesus said critics had linked him with Satan, and the disciples should not expect any less criticism for themselves. For sure, we are to be like Jesus in all the positive ways, but disciples of any generation should not be surprised at difficult times, even within their own families. Jesus warned them he was sending them out as "sheep among wolves" (10:16–23). Earlier, in the Beatitudes, Jesus taught the disciples about persecution and God's reward for those who are faithful (5:8–10).

Jesus was up-front with his disciples. Critics, even those who professed to be God's people, hounded Jesus until they crucified him. Our hope is that we will not have to endure any form of persecution or crucifixion for our faithfulness, but Jesus has warned us. Bad things may happen while we are on God's mission. That comes with the human package of freedom and faith, but we face life with the grace of God that is sufficient for every need any disciple has (2 Corinthians 12:9).

Matthew 10:26–31 speaks clearly about fear: "So do not be afraid of them." Although the critics were numerous, Jesus saw no reason for disciples to be muzzled. Jesus empowered his disciples and told them, *go, preach, and heal.* The word is clear; don't be afraid of anyone who tries to inhibit your speaking about Jesus or your ministry in the name of

DISCIPLES AND APOSTLES

Jesus selected twelve men to have a key role in the development of the church. They were known as disciples and apostles. For three years, these disciples walked with Jesus and learned from and about him. After the Gospels and Acts 1, the only disciples mentioned prominently are Simon Peter, John, and James. Later legends about the disciples cannot be verified.

After the resurrection of Jesus, *apostle* became the most common term for the twelve disciples. Apostle means *one who is sent.* Matthew used the noun form once (Matt. 10:2). The verb form is found in Matthew 10:5 and 10:16, where the disciples were sent on a mission. Later in the New Testament, we find other apostles mentioned, including these: Matthias (Acts 1:26), Paul, Barnabas (Acts 14:14), Andronicus (Rom. 16:7), Junia (Rom. 16:7), and "James, the Lord's brother" (Galatians 1:19; see also 1 Cor. 9:5). Only once do we see an effort to keep the number of apostles to twelve (Acts 1:12–26).

Today we need both qualities: discipleship (an obedient learner) and apostleship (going out with the message of Jesus). Doing both, we continue to do the mission that Jesus began.

Jesus. Jesus taught the disciples in private but now said for them to tell it all publicly. The one who came to reveal God had nothing to hide, and God's truth does not need to be hidden. Truth ultimately endures and prevails.

Matthew 10:28 identifies one fear that is real, fear of God. *Fear* is used in the Bible to describe great wonder and reverence for God, for God is awesome. Yet, there are times when fear simply means we should be afraid of God. God is the ultimate reference point to whom we must adjust our lives (see Rom. 14:12). As such, God is a God of judgment and love. Some strangely think that Jesus implied we are to fear Satan, but in the Bible, Satan is not to be feared but resisted. James wrote that when you do that, Satan flees (James 4:7). Only God controls the destiny of your body and soul.

Although we may not escape suffering and persecution, we are assured that each disciple of Jesus is special in the sight of God. Hyperbole is

---

Reaching Your Neighborhood

- Pray for how you and others can extend the ministry of Jesus to those not connected to the church.
- Ask your pastor to help you become a better recruiter for Jesus.
- Enlist others to walk along with you in this journey of discipleship and outreach.
- Do not be afraid to speak to someone, Christian or non-Christian, every day about spiritual matters.
- If someone is indifferent or rejects you, *shake the dust off your feet*, but keep going and talking.
- Do not be filled with ego or frustrated with results. Let the Lord be the Lord of the harvest.
- Remember how much God really cares for you and others.

---

a good way to understand Jesus' illustrations about sparrows and hair. Hyperbole is a literary device that uses an obvious overstatement to make a point. Jesus is not saying God has a heavenly scoreboard to count birds and hair. The point is: God cares about sparrows, and you are far more special than a little bird. You are far more precious to God than a hair, and you are not a number. The point is: if God cares about these things we think are small and insignificant, how much more does God care for you? As you are going about, share this with others so that they also can know that God truly cares for them and offers them a life that really matters. As the poet John Greenleaf Whittier (1807–1892) wrote,[1]

> I know not where His islands lift,
> Their fronded palms in air,
> I only know I cannot drift
> Beyond His love and care.

This Lesson and Life

Matthew 11:1 closes the second major teaching section of Matthew with "after Jesus had finished instructing his twelve disciples." The Greek word used here for "instructing" is not a common word for instructing and is often translated *command*. Jesus was *commanding* the disciples to act. Jesus gave these instructions because he wanted the disciples to *do* them.

Feelings are special. I'm grateful for emotion and feeling, for if nothing else, it means I'm still alive. Spiritually speaking, however, are you a feeling person or a commandment person? Do you follow the teachings of Jesus when you feel like it or because God commands them?

We've heard a lot about God working in the world. If you really want to know where God is working in our world, follow his commands. They will lead you to him and to his (and your) mission in the world.

QUESTIONS

1. If you rated yourself on being an extension of the teaching, preaching, and healing ministry of Jesus, how would you evaluate yourself?

2. Are you involved in the mission and ministry of Jesus in a way that causes you to discipline your time and money? Be specific.

3. How can past failures or fear impact your life as a disciple of Jesus Christ?

4. What do you think the saying, *We have fearlessness that grows out of fear,* suggests about a person's relationship to non-Christians?

5. What are you deliberately doing that helps others experience the love of God?

NOTES ———————————————————————————————————

1. John Greenleaf Whittier, "The Eternal Goodness," in Frank Mead, *Encyclopedia of Religious Quotations* (Westbrook, New Jersey: Fleming H. Revell Company), 190. See http://whittier.classicauthors.net/PoemsOfJohnGreenleafWhittier/ PoemsOfJohnGreenleafWhittier1.html. Accessed 4/4/11.

Believing Means Following

FOCAL TEXT
Matthew 16:13–17, 21–26

BACKGROUND
Matthew 16:13–26

MAIN IDEA
Truly believing in Jesus means following Jesus no matter the cost.

QUESTION TO EXPLORE
How much do you believe in Jesus?

STUDY AIM
To decide to express my belief in Jesus by following him

QUICK READ
Jesus told his disciples that following him would cost them everything. Every person who follows Jesus should expect to make sacrifices.

A college friend, Paul, took literally Jesus' words, "If anyone would come after me, he must deny himself and take up his cross and follow me" (Matthew 16:24). My friend designed a wooden cross, with a wheel at the bottom, to carry on his back as he walked from town to town. Paul was quickly noticed in each town, and people would respond to him in various ways. Some people thought he was weird, but many people listened to his story about why he carried the cross. Paul paid a physical and emotional price to follow Jesus in this way. However, it also gave him a unique way to share the love of Jesus.

Obviously Jesus did not intend for all of us to design a wooden cross and carry it around on our backs. However, Jesus did make clear that following him is costly. It may cost us some privileges our world has to offer, it may cost us financially, it may cost us worldly success, and in extreme cases, it may cost us our lives. Therefore, we must expect to pay a price ourselves, and we must inform others that following Jesus requires commitment and sacrifice.

MATTHEW 16:13–17, 21–26

¹³ When Jesus came to the region of Caesarea Philippi, he asked his disciples, "Who do people say the Son of Man is?"

¹⁴ They replied, "Some say John the Baptist; others say Elijah; and still others, Jeremiah or one of the prophets."

¹⁵ "But what about you?" he asked. "Who do you say I am?"

¹⁶ Simon Peter answered, "You are the Christ, the Son of the living God."

¹⁷ Jesus replied, "Blessed are you, Simon son of Jonah, for this was not revealed to you by man, but by my Father in heaven.

. . . .

²¹ From that time on Jesus began to explain to his disciples that he must go to Jerusalem and suffer many things at the hands of the elders, chief priests and teachers of the law, and that he must be killed and on the third day be raised to life.

²² Peter took him aside and began to rebuke him. "Never, Lord!" he said. "This shall never happen to you!"

> ²³ Jesus turned and said to Peter, "Get behind me, Satan! You are a stumbling block to me; you do not have in mind the things of God, but the things of men."
>
> ²⁴ Then Jesus said to his disciples, "If anyone would come after me, he must deny himself and take up his cross and follow me. ²⁵ For whoever wants to save his life will lose it, but whoever loses his life for me will find it. ²⁶ What good will it be for a man if he gains the whole world, yet forfeits his soul? Or what can a man give in exchange for his soul?

What's the Word on the Street (16:13–14)

In his Gospel, Matthew recorded that Jesus was walking and talking with his disciples in a region known as Caesarea Philippi. This region, located north-northeast of the Sea of Galilee, was inhabited mostly by Gentiles. One of Herod the Great's three sons, Philip, governed this region. Philip took over when he was sixteen years old and reigned for thirty-seven years. Caesarea Philippi was an important Greco-Roman city; the residents included pagan Syrians and Greeks. Its name gave honor to Caesar Augustus. Later the name of Philip was added to honor him and to distinguish this city from the other city named Caesarea.

Caesarea Philippi was notorious for its pagan worship. Baal, the Greek god Pan, and Caesar were among its leading gods and idols. The city contained many different shrines and monuments to false religions. In an environment filled with pagan symbols, Jesus asked his disciples several questions.

Jesus asked his disciples what other people were saying about him. Jesus had not yet revealed himself as Messiah; he commonly referred to himself as the Son of Man. The names the disciples listed were all prophets. Jews believed the Messiah would be a great prophet. The disciples reported that some people thought he was John the Baptist come back to life. Others believed Jesus was Elijah because it was prophesied that Elijah would come again. Still others believed Jesus was Jeremiah, the weeping prophet. Like Jeremiah, Jesus wept over the condition of God's people. Each prophet listed by the disciples fit one of the popular beliefs about the Messiah.

What Do You Think? (16:15–17)

After the disciples told Jesus what others said about him, Jesus asked, "Who do you say I am?" This question highlights the point that the important question is not what others say about Jesus but rather what we believe about Jesus. Scripture teaches that every person will one day give an answer regarding Jesus' identity (Romans 14:12). The decisions of a group of people can never substitute for one's personal decision.

Peter, a spokesperson for the group, made a crucial statement about Jesus' identity. Although others had proclaimed that Jesus was the Son of God before Peter's confession (John 1:49; Matt. 14:33), this was the first time the title "Christ" was used to address Jesus directly. The title in the Greek language means *anointed* or *anointed one*. It was used in the Old Testament more than thirty-five times but only for kings, priests, or prophets, usually for people who had been anointed with oil. Jesus accepted this title, and he knew God the Father had revealed this to Peter. God hid the truth about Jesus from the proud religious leaders but revealed it to the humble disciples.

Peter also stated that Jesus was "the Son of the living God." In contrast to the statues and monuments to the mythical gods, Jesus belonged to the only God who is alive and active. This statement pointed to the fact that Jesus is uniquely God's Son. Peter's words also revealed the culmination of all the teachings and experiences Jesus had with his

RELIGIOUS RULERS

Jesus told his disciples that he would be handed over to the elders, chief priests, and teachers of the law (Matt. 16:21). Together, these groups made up the ruling leadership of Jerusalem. The title *elders* was given to men who were of age and experience and held a position of leadership among the Pharisees and Sadducees. The ruling aristocracy over Judea was known as the *chief priests.* During Jesus' time on earth, these chief priests came from four prominent families who ruled over Jewish affairs. They were responsible for filling the positions of priest, captain, and treasurers of the temple. The *scribes*, also known as *teachers of the law*, interpreted the law. They were closely connected to the Pharisees.

disciples. Because of this revelation, Jesus could move his disciples into a deeper understanding of who he was and what God sent him to do.

The Rewards of the Right Answer (16:18–20)

Jesus stated that Peter was blessed because he received this revelation from God. Jesus called Simon by the name *Peter* (Greek *petros*), which means a *rock*. Then Jesus stated that on this rock he would build his church. The word he used for *rock* the second time was *petra,* and it means *large rock.* He did not intend that Peter himself would be the foundation of the church but rather that Jesus would build his church on the foundation of Jesus' true identity, proclaimed by Peter.

Jesus also informed Peter and the other disciples that they would receive "the keys of the kingdom of heaven" (Matt. 16:19). Jesus knew that after his ascension to heaven, these men would be responsible to carry the gospel to the ends of the earth. Once the doors of the gospel were open to all nations, there would be no more need for keys. People who receive the gospel are loosed from the power and penalty of sin. People who reject the gospel are bound by their sins and cannot enter into the kingdom of heaven.

Know When to Stop Talking (16:21–23)

Matthew demonstrated that after Jesus made his identity known, he started to make his purpose known. Matthew recorded three other times Jesus informed his disciples of his arrest and crucifixion (17:22–23; 20:17–19; 26:2). Although Jesus told his disciples that he would be crucified, they still believed he would be a revolutionary liberator for God's people. Peter, filled with the confidence of God's blessing and Jesus' words of affirmation, spoke for the other disciples and declared that no harm would come to Jesus. In a Jewish master-disciple relationship, the disciple dared not correct, much less rebuke, his master. When Peter called Jesus "Lord" (16:22), he seems to have been using the title as merely a respectful human address. This indicated he still did not see Jesus as Master but more as a human authority. Peter had enough faith to proclaim Jesus as the Christ, but he did not have enough faith to submit to

God's will and let Jesus suffer and die. If we are prepared to trust Jesus during times of blessing, we must also be prepared to trust Jesus during times of suffering. As Job said to his wife after they lost their children and their livestock and Job's body was covered in boils, "Shall we accept good from God, and not trouble?" (Job 2:10). Peter had his own thoughts about the path Jesus should follow; however, all disciples must submit to God's plans over their own.

Jesus rebuked Peter and called him Satan in order to emphasize that Peter was harboring Satan's thoughts rather than God's. Satan wanted to stop Jesus from completing his mission. Earlier in the conversation, God had revealed Jesus' identity to Peter, and he proclaimed it publicly. Moments later Peter was listening to the voice of Satan when he attempted to disrupt Jesus' mission. Peter demonstrated how quickly a disciple can be persuaded by the enemy. Jesus took this opportunity to tell his followers what it would cost to be his disciple.

Listen to the Answer (16:24–26)

Jesus informed his disciples that they would need to take up their own cross to follow him. The image of the cross in the first century was a dark image that signified a slow and painful death. Crucifixion was one of the most painful and shameful ways to die. The Romans used this method of execution to deter anyone who might want to rebel against Rome. Criminals sentenced to be crucified were often made to carry the crossbeam of the cross on their backs to the place of the crucifixion.

INNER CITY

Mario gave his life to Jesus at age thirty-four, and immediately God called him into ministry. Mario and his wife began to pray and ask God to tell them where they should minister. They both felt God calling them back to the inner city, a place they had worked so hard to leave. Although God had given them a heart to reach inner-city people, they were concerned about raising their family in that culture. How would you advise Mario and his wife regarding God's call back to the inner city?

Once they arrived, soldiers nailed the criminals to the crossbeam and hoisted it in the air. Jesus was not referring to the cross as the burdens or problems a person must carry. Rather, to take up one's cross meant to identify with the rejection, shame, suffering, and death of Jesus.

Jesus emphasized the cost of discipleship on one's life and soul. The kingdom of God is a reverse kingdom from worldly kingdoms. What is normal to humans is not normal to God. Jesus made it clear to his disciples that what is required to follow God is not reserved for certain times of life but for every day. If we work hard to hang on to and control our lives, we will actually lose them. By controlling our lives, we reject what God desires for us. On the other hand, if we will forsake our self-centered desires and accept God's desires for our life, we experience salvation and righteousness.

To trade one's spiritual existence for the pleasures of the world ultimately leads to death. The word "exchange" expresses something priceless (16:26). Jesus pointed to the blessing that comes when a person realizes the value of salvation compared to the value of earthly things. What the world has to offer cannot match the richness of obedience to Christ.

Applying This Lesson to Life

Every day we are encouraged to get the most out of life. That is a great idea; however, Christ's disciples get the most out of life when they glorify God with their lives. A great question we should ask before we make a decision or complete an action is this, *Is this going to bring glory to me or to God?* Many times giving glory to God requires us to give up or change something in our lives.

QUESTIONS

1. What are some ideas people have about Jesus today?

2. Jesus praised Peter when he proclaimed Jesus to be the Christ. Moments later, Jesus rebuked him and called him "Satan." What lessons can we gain from how quickly Peter went from listening to God to being persuaded by Satan?

3. In what ways have you denied yourself in order to follow Jesus?

4. Why would a person not want to follow Christ?

5. How has following Jesus made your life better?

FOCAL TEXT
Matthew 23:1–12

BACKGROUND
Matthew 23:1–36

MAIN IDEA

Disciples of Jesus are to practice their faith with genuineness, grace, and humility.

QUESTION TO EXPLORE

Why do religious people sometimes become hypocritical, harsh, and arrogant—lacking in true discipleship?

STUDY AIM

To identify ways I need to put these teachings of Jesus into practice in my life

QUICK READ

Jesus pointed out that many of the Pharisees and other religious leaders were not serving God but serving self. In contrast, Jesus taught that a true disciple demonstrates grace and humility.

LESSON TWELVE

Be Genuine, Show Grace, Be Humble

Ryan wanted to plug into his new church, and so the pastor asked him to teach a class of children. His first Sunday to teach was the Sunday before Thanksgiving. To get to know the kids, Ryan asked them to introduce themselves and tell one thing for which they were thankful.

Something about one girl suggested she was less fortunate than the other kids. She said her name was Abigail and she was thankful for free breakfasts at school. Ryan could hardly choke back the tears. Ryan found out Abigail lived with her mom in a tiny one-bedroom apartment, and her mom worked two jobs just to make ends meet.

Ryan made arrangements with the mom and delivered a full Thanksgiving meal to Abigail's apartment. As Ryan finished unloading the food, he heard Abigail ask her mom whether Ryan was Jesus.

The mom replied, "Why do you ask?"

Abigail said, "You always tell me Jesus loves us, and this man obviously loves us, so is he Jesus?"

The mom replied, "Well sweetie, I guess he is Jesus."

MATTHEW 23:1–12

[1] Then Jesus said to the crowds and to his disciples: [2] "The teachers of the law and the Pharisees sit in Moses' seat. [3] So you must obey them and do everything they tell you. But do not do what they do, for they do not practice what they preach. [4] They tie up heavy loads and put them on men's shoulders, but they themselves are not willing to lift a finger to move them.

[5] "Everything they do is done for men to see: They make their phylacteries wide and the tassels on their garments long; [6] they love the place of honor at banquets and the most important seats in the synagogues; [7] they love to be greeted in the marketplaces and to have men call them 'Rabbi.'

[8] "But you are not to be called 'Rabbi,' for you have only one Master and you are all brothers. [9] And do not call anyone on earth 'father,' for you have one Father, and he is in heaven. [10] Nor are you to be called 'teacher,' for you have one Teacher, the Christ. [11] The greatest among you will be your servant. [12] For whoever exalts himself will be humbled, and whoever humbles himself will be exalted.

Practice What You Preach (23:1–4)

Most people living in Jesus' day were not well educated. Others, such as the Pharisees and the teachers of the law, were well educated. This difference gave religious leaders the ability to overwhelm the common people. These leaders would impose certain rules and regulations on the people as a form of control. Jesus pointed out that these leaders assumed authority not given them by God.

Jesus stated that these leaders sat in Moses' seat and the people were to obey what the teachers told them as long as what they taught was Scripture. (A rabbi sat on a chair in the synagogue when he taught, which represented the place of authority. Archeological evidence has uncovered stone seats for people of authority in the synagogue.) The word of God was the only authority Jesus recognized. He did not recognize the traditions and rules designed by the Pharisees. Jesus never condemned the Pharisees for teaching the law of God, but he did expose their corruption when they incorrectly interpreted it.

Jesus warned the people not to follow the Pharisees' example. People will rarely listen to us if our life does not match up with what we say. It is possible to do the right things for the wrong reasons and therefore discredit ourselves. The Pharisees were so preoccupied with outward righteousness that they ignored inward character and integrity. God desires inward and outward obedience from his followers.

Pharisees lived according to a double standard. They put heavy burdens on the people while they sought to lighten their own load. In addition to teaching the law of Moses, Pharisees handed down oral law. They used this law to interpret and apply the law of Moses, the *Torah*. It was here that the Pharisees added more laws that oppressed the people.

In contrast, Jesus did everything he asked his followers to do. He came to lighten the burden, not add to it.

Don't Be a Showoff (23:5–7)

Jesus condemned the Pharisees for trying to make the headlines every time they did something. One gets the feeling that if the paparazzi had existed in those days, the Pharisees would have them around all the time. They sought glory and recognition.

The Pharisees worked hard to look religious. Even the clothes they wore reflected their arrogance. Phylacteries were small leather boxes men wore on their left arm and forehead during morning worship. The boxes contained Scripture written on parchment. This tradition was in keeping with Deuteronomy 6:8 and 11:18. In addition to the phylacteries, men wore a robe that contained four tassels. The tassels were reminders for the people to be holy by keeping the entire law. They wore these tassels in keeping with the law (see Numbers 15:38). However, the Pharisees made "their phylacteries wide and the tassels on their garments long" (Matt. 23:5b).

Jesus also criticized the Pharisees because they sought to place themselves in positions of honor. The host of a party would seat people in order based on status and importance. The place of highest honor was to the right of the host. The second place of honor was to the host's left.

In the synagogue, people sat on benches or mats. Certain benches or chairs were designated for people of prominence. "Moses' seat" was reserved for the person speaking on the Scriptures (23:2).

Don't Wear Your Title (23:8–10)

Jesus pointed out that "the teachers of the law and the Pharisees" took their desire for recognition beyond seating arrangements to the way people addressed them. They loved for people to call them "rabbi." The term "rabbi" meant *my great one*. A rabbi was a master teacher of the law and usually the leader of a school. The schools focused on the study of the *Torah*, the law of Moses, the first five books of the Bible.

Jesus warned his disciples not to use three specific titles: rabbi, father, and teacher. A disciple of a rabbi sought to eventually become a rabbi. A disciple of Jesus would always be a disciple, never a master. Jesus would always be the Master, the ultimate authority. The disciples were equal, like brothers.

The term "father" represented honor, authority, and respect. It was used among religious leaders to refer to heads of the rabbinic court and esteemed scholars and rabbis. The warning against using the title "father" for a spiritual leader reiterated that God is the only spiritual Father. If all disciples were brothers, they also had a common spiritual

Father. Jesus warned his disciples not to place people in the place of authority that belonged to God alone.

The term "teacher" denoted a private tutor. A private teacher held authority over a student. Disciples of Jesus were not to seek authority over other people. Although teachers existed, true spiritual teachers led people to closer relationships with God; they did not seek to replace God. Jesus alone held personal authority over his disciples. Jesus encouraged his disciples to think more of others and less about themselves.

It says a lot about a person and how the person sees his or her role if the person demands other people call them by their title. That includes ministers.

A New Leadership Model (23:11–12)

Again we see that following Jesus is counter to our culture. The world says we can measure success by how many people are under us; Jesus said we are successful when we serve others. These verses echo Jesus' earlier statement that he is the example of greatness in God's kingdom (Matt. 20:26–28). The Pharisees wanted to manufacture greatness by

PHYLACTERIES

Excavators discovered leather boxes called phylacteries while digging in the archaeological site known as Qumran. This site is famous because of its proximity to the caves where archaeologists discovered the Dead Sea Scrolls. One box was approximately an inch long and contained four compartments, which contained four tiny scrolls. The scrolls were made out of parchment and contained verses from Exodus 13:9, 16; and Deuteronomy 6:8; 11:18. The other box was approximately one-third of an inch long and contained one compartment with all four verses written on one scroll. This phylactery was worn on the left arm. Regulations prohibited rabbis from making the boxes too big to keep the rabbis from looking too pious. The practice of wearing phylacteries came from Deuteronomy 6:4–8, where Moses instructed the Israelites to teach their children God's commandments and to tie them on their hands and foreheads.

their position and their reputation. The Pharisees were power hungry leaders who felt their position allowed them to control people. They wanted to keep the people humble while they gained authority.

In contrast to the Pharisees, who adopted a worldly model of leadership, a disciple of Jesus must exhibit servant leadership. Jesus made it clear that God would humble disciples who worked to make their name great by exerting authority over others, but God would applaud disciples who dedicated their lives to serving others. Vain glory will last only a season, but God's glory is eternal. God removed the role the Pharisees held in addition to taking away their leadership positions. God called disciples who served others sons and daughters of the kingdom. These same brothers and sisters also enjoyed equality with one another, with Jesus as their Teacher and God as their Father.

Applying This Lesson to Life

Jesus made clear to his disciples that following him is a lifelong process. Disciples are to be constantly developing, growing, and learning what following Jesus means and costs. Denying ourselves is a daily experience as we put God's will before our own. People who call themselves Christians but do not exhibit the character of Jesus are either mistaken about their identity in Christ or have forgotten what it takes to follow Jesus.

When we spend time talking to Jesus and reading the Scriptures, we naturally become more like him. Have you ever noticed that the longer we are with our spouse or a close friend, the more we talk or act like that person? The same is true with our relationship with Jesus. The more time we spend with Jesus, the more we sound and act like him.

CASE STUDY

Morgan is a children's minister. Recently the church called a new pastor, and he wants the staff to call him pastor in public. She also noticed that in public the pastor is warm and friendly; around the office he is cold and demanding. All of this has a negative effect on the staff. How can Morgan respond to the new pastor with grace and humility?

Many of the Pharisees were caught up in doing religion; therefore, they missed having a relationship with God's Son. As a disciple, our goal is not to do more religious stuff but rather to enjoy, relax, and understand what it is to be in Christ. At that point, Christ's personality shows in us.

QUESTIONS

1. What are some actions or attitudes you have had lately that could fit under the category, *living like a Pharisee?*

2. What are some recent temptations you faced to think more like your culture than like a disciple?

3. What are some examples of religious arrogance you have witnessed?

4. Why did Jesus warn his disciples against seeking the titles of
   rabbi, father, and master?

5. What are some things you have done to humble yourself?

6. How have you demonstrated servant leadership lately?

———— U N I T   F O U R ————

Following Jesus' Command

Unit four, "Following Jesus' Command," consists of one lesson on Jesus' command, "Make disciples," in Matthew 28:16–20. The lesson emphasizes that these verses called "The Great Commission" are a command, not a suggestion. The lesson stresses that the responsibility Jesus gave us is to "make disciples."

FOCAL TEXT
Matthew 28:16–20

BACKGROUND
Matthew 28:16–20

MAIN IDEA
Jesus commands his disciples
to make disciples of all people.

QUESTION TO EXPLORE
If you and your church were
as serious as Jesus is in the
command, "make disciples,"
what would you do?

STUDY AIM
To describe what Jesus'
command to "make disciples"
means and decide on actions
I will take to be more
faithful in carrying it out

QUICK READ
Jesus commanded all who
follow him to be intentional
about making disciples. True
disciples understand Jesus
wants us to devote our lives to
sharing our faith with others.

LESSON THIRTEEN
A Command, Not a Suggestion

A Pharisee once asked Jesus: "Teacher, which is the greatest commandment in the Law?" Jesus replied, "Love the Lord your God with all your heart and with all your soul and with all your mind." He then stated that the second greatest commandment is like the first: "Love your neighbor as yourself" (Matthew 22:34–39). These two commandments are sometimes referred to as the *Great Commandment.*

Jesus made another statement that is commonly referred to as the Great Commission: "Therefore go and make disciples of all nations, baptizing them in the name of the Father and of the Son and of the Holy Spirit, and teaching them to obey everything I have commanded you" (Matt. 28:19–20). It is interesting to note that the Great Commandment and the Great Commission go hand in hand. If we love God, then we will love people. If we love people, we will be diligent in making them disciples. How do we make people disciples? This session is designed to answer that question.

Matthew recorded five discourses that alternate with narratives of Jesus' life. Matthew arranged them in such a way as to create a handbook for discipleship. Matthew recorded the teachings and training methods of Jesus so disciples in the first century and centuries to follow might be trained as well. Matthew noted that Jesus did more than just teach his disciples; he modeled what he taught. Matthew further emphasized Jesus' focus on the need for disciple-making by including one of Jesus' last conversations with his disciples, a conversation in which Jesus commanded his followers to make disciples. The verses in this lesson's text show that true discipleship is first birthed out of worship of God.

MATTHEW 28:16–20

[16] Then the eleven disciples went to Galilee, to the mountain where Jesus had told them to go. [17] When they saw him, they worshiped him; but some doubted. [18] Then Jesus came to them and said, "All authority in heaven and on earth has been given to me. [19] Therefore go and make disciples of all nations, baptizing them in the name of the Father and of the Son and of the Holy Spirit, [20] and teaching them to obey everything I have commanded you. And surely I am with you always, to the very end of the age."

Jesus Appeared to His Disciples (28:16–17)

Matthew reported that the eleven disciples went to a mountain in Galilee where Jesus told them to meet. This was the first time the disciples were called "the eleven" (28:16). By this time, Judas Iscariot had killed himself, but Matthias had not yet been added to take his place (Acts 1). When Jesus was arrested, all the disciples, with the exception of Peter, fled. However, Peter publicly denied knowing Jesus; therefore, he too was guilty of abandoning Jesus.

Now, the eleven disciples were reunited. Jesus had told them before his death that he would die and rise again and go before them into Galilee (26:32). They were told again by the angel and by Jesus after the resurrection that he would meet them there (28:7, 10). It is not clear on which mountain the disciples gathered, only that it was in Galilee. Obviously the spot was familiar to the disciples; Galilee was the region where they had ministered alongside Jesus. That the area was called "Galilee of the Gentiles" (4:15) further reinforces Jesus' instructions that the disciples were to go into all the nations to make disciples. The Spirit of God would eventually lead the disciples to take the gospel to the Gentiles.

Matthew recorded two post-resurrection appearances of Jesus to his followers. Jesus first appeared to the women at the tomb on the morning of the resurrection (28:9–10), and later to the disciples on the mountain in Galilee. From John's Gospel, we know that Jesus had already appeared to the disciples in a locked room (John 20:19). Therefore, they had already seen Jesus and knew he was alive. The eleven and perhaps others worshiped Jesus when he appeared.

Matthew 28:17 states, "When they saw him, they worshiped him; but some doubted." It stands to reason that those who doubted were other followers who had not yet encountered the risen Jesus. The eleven disciples doubted Jesus' resurrection until they encountered him face-to-face. A common human response is to demand proof to believe something that we thought impossible. Matthew may have been alluding to the group of more than five hundred people Jesus appeared to before he ascended to heaven (1 Corinthians 15:6).

Jesus Sent His Disciples (28:18–20)

The last verses of Matthew's Gospel boldly confess the message of the entire book. They highlight the reason Jesus came to earth, to establish the kingdom of God in the hearts of people. In these last verses, Jesus commissioned his disciples to go and make more of the same. Jesus spent the last three years of his life on earth training and empowering his disciples; here Jesus commissioned them to do likewise. However, their commission went far beyond the region of Galilee; it was to the ends of the earth.

Matthew devoted much of his writings to the authority of Jesus. It is fitting that he would include Jesus' statement that all authority was given to him. Authority is the right to use power. Jesus had it, and he gave it to his followers at this point. Knowing Jesus was still in control and that he had all authority brought security and meaning to the disciples. Here Jesus delegated this authority to his disciples.

After Jesus affirmed his authority, he told his disciples to go and make disciples. The word "go" is a Greek participle that means *going*.

Z. N. MORRELL

In 1835, a preacher from Tennessee named Z. N. Morrell arrived in Texas. Health issues had caused him to leave the climate of Tennessee for a warmer and gentler Texas climate. On arriving in Texas, Pastor Morrell began looking for opportunity to serve and spread the gospel in Texas.

Times were difficult. In 1839, Sam Houston was about to leave office. Mexicans, American Indians, and Texans were battling one another. The church in Washington, Texas, had been dissolved. Frustrated, weary, and discouraged, Reverend Morrell moved just outside LaGrange and started conducting church services. Soon a man named R. E. B. Baylor showed up in town, and Reverend Morrell enlisted his help with the new church that met at Plum Grove. Baylor was a source of strength and energy for Morrell. Finally, in March of 1839, Morrell baptized his first convert. That opened the door for many more baptisms in the months to follow. Reverend Morrell followed the call of God to Texas, and God gave him success in reaching people in a new land.[1]

The intent was that as they lived their lives they were to make disciples. This indicated a life focus as well as intentionality. Wherever the disciples went or whatever they did, Jesus wanted them to make disciples.

"Make disciples" is the primary command in the Great Commission. It is the only imperative. The words translated "go," "baptizing," and "teaching" are participles, and they speak to the process of making disciples. When a person responded to the call to follow Jesus, the disciples were to baptize that person and then train the person to respond in obedience to the teachings of Jesus. Therefore, disciples of Jesus would be people who believed in Jesus as the Messiah and expressed faith through baptism and commitment to the fellowship of other believers. In addition to these commitments, new disciples were also commissioned to go and make more disciples. The early church grew using this method. Following Christ meant more than securing personal salvation; it also included willingness and a practice of seeking out people for the purpose of making more disciples. Once the disciples led people to accept the truth about Jesus, they were to teach them "to obey everything I have commanded you" (28:20).

Jesus broke many barriers by the way he made disciples. He broke gender, ethnic, religious, economic, and social barriers. A disciple of Jesus did not look to the church, the Pharisees, or any other prophet for salvation. A true disciple found eternal life in Jesus alone. Once a person accepted the truth about Jesus, the disciples were to teach and train that person.

The name the angels gave Jesus at his birth, Immanuel, means "God with us" (1:23). In the Great Commission, Jesus reiterated the promise of his presence when he told his disciples he would go with them to the end of the age.

In this promise, Jesus proclaimed his deity. A Jew believed that only God was eternal and omnipresent. Jesus told his followers that he would be with them through every step of the disciple-making process. He would be with them as they went to the various nations proclaiming the gospel. He would be with the new disciples. He would be present as new disciples matured. He would be present as the church grew. He would be present with the eleven disciples as they themselves matured in their discipleship. Jesus gave his disciples all the necessary resources, including himself, to fulfill the Great Commission.

DISCIPLE

We must *be* disciples in order to *make* disciples. Here are some steps to help in making disciples:

- Define and write out a plan to use to mentor someone as a disciple. Do not make it up as you go.
- Help disciples make clear decisions about moving ahead.
- Give disciples a glimpse of what they can become.
- Model what you are teaching.
- Spend the majority of the time encouraging the disciple.
- Be open to sharing your life with the disciple.
- Pray daily for the disciple.

Jesus would be with his disciples to the end of the age. Jesus' presence assured his followers that the world was not out of control. His promise also granted courage and power to proclaim the good news even to hostile people who would reject the truth. Just as Jesus walked with his disciples on earth, he would walk with them intimately and faithfully in the present and future.

Applying This Lesson to Life

When Jesus ascended to heaven after his resurrection, he commissioned his followers to carry on the mission he started. There is no Plan B. Every disciple has the same charge—"make disciples."

Following Jesus is a life-long process. So is making disciples. Here are two questions to constantly ask ourselves: *Who is teaching me? Who am I teaching to follow Jesus?* At any given time we should have a mentor in the faith and be mentoring someone. A great model for disciple-making is to take the experience, learning, and testimony of one follower of Christ and share it with another believer to help that person follow Jesus.

QUESTIONS

1. If the Holy Spirit calls people to repentance, why did Jesus put such an emphasis on us to make disciples?

2. What specific actions are you taking today to develop as a disciple of Jesus?

3. What adjustments or changes do you need to make to become more devoted as a disciple of Jesus?

4. What programs or ministries does your church have to make disciples? to help people develop as disciples?

5. What can you do to help your church make and train disciples?

NOTES

1. Z. N. Morell, *Flowers and Fruits in the Wilderness* (Saint Louis: Commercial Printing Company, 1872), 53–56.

FOCAL TEXT
Luke 2:1–20

BACKGROUND
Luke 2:1–20

MAIN IDEA

Truly understanding the meaning of God's sending Jesus leads to responding with obedient action.

QUESTION TO EXPLORE

What action does God's sending Jesus call for?

STUDY AIM

To explain the meaning of God's sending Jesus and decide how I will respond with my life

QUICK READ

Jesus was born to be the Savior, Christ the Lord, with only his parents and animals to share in the first moments. The shepherds who saw him first were also the first to tell others about Jesus.

CHRISTMAS LESSON
Going to Bethlehem

Childbirth has never been easy. At the end of a long and challenging nine months, a mother gives birth to her child. In recent decades, the father is now with the mother at the time of birth, often coaching her through the pains of labor. Other family may be in the room. When the baby is delivered, normally tears of joy and celebration are shared. Everything about the birthing room is designed to make the birthing experience as clean, easy, and happy as possible.

Jesus' birth had no comforts available, and hygiene was minimal. His first nights were spent sleeping in a feeding trough for animals. Although it was common to have a mid-wife or experienced woman to help the mother at birth, no mention is made in the Scriptures of anyone else being present other than Mary and Joseph. No family assisted; no family or friends were present to share in the moment. God and his angels promised the experience; they saw the new family through.

LUKE 2:1–20

1 In those days Caesar Augustus issued a decree that a census should be taken of the entire Roman world. 2 (This was the first census that took place while Quirinius was governor of Syria.) 3 And everyone went to his own town to register.

4 So Joseph also went up from the town of Nazareth in Galilee to Judea, to Bethlehem the town of David, because he belonged to the house and line of David. 5 He went there to register with Mary, who was pledged to be married to him and was expecting a child. 6 While they were there, the time came for the baby to be born, 7 and she gave birth to her firstborn, a son. She wrapped him in cloths and placed him in a manger, because there was no room for them in the inn.

8 And there were shepherds living out in the fields nearby, keeping watch over their flocks at night. 9 An angel of the Lord appeared to them, and the glory of the Lord shone around them, and they were terrified. 10 But the angel said to them, "Do not be afraid. I bring you good news of great joy that will be for all the people. 11 Today in the town of David a Savior has been born to you; he is Christ the Lord. 12 This will be a sign to you: You will find a baby wrapped in cloths and lying in a manger."

¹³ Suddenly a great company of the heavenly host appeared with the angel, praising God and saying,

¹⁴ "Glory to God in the highest, and on earth peace to men on whom his favor rests."

¹⁵ When the angels had left them and gone into heaven, the shepherds said to one another, "Let's go to Bethlehem and see this thing that has happened, which the Lord has told us about."

¹⁶ So they hurried off and found Mary and Joseph, and the baby, who was lying in the manger. ¹⁷ When they had seen him, they spread the word concerning what had been told them about this child, ¹⁸ and all who heard it were amazed at what the shepherds said to them. ¹⁹ But Mary treasured up all these things and pondered them in her heart. ²⁰ The shepherds returned, glorifying and praising God for all the things they had heard and seen, which were just as they had been told.

The Birth of Jesus (2:1–7)

Jesus' parents were ordinary, common people from a small town in Israel. Emperors and governors were unaware of them. Religious leaders may have known them in Nazareth, but they had no privileged status for travel or lodging. Yet God chose them for their unique experience in history.

Luke wrote that angels visited Elizabeth and Zechariah, the expectant parents of John the Baptist. God had done a miracle in Elizabeth's life, a woman who had the nickname of "the barren one" (Luke 1:36). She became pregnant in her old age, and her pregnancy would encourage Mary in her miraculous pregnancy. Mary also was visited by an angel (1:26–38) and told that she, an unmarried virgin, would give birth to a son, the Messiah of Israel. Mary wondered "How will this be since I am a virgin?" The angel said, "Nothing is impossible with God." Mary's classic response of faith was, "I am the Lord's servant. . . . May it be to me as you have said" (1:38).

As this was going on with Mary, Matthew wrote that an angel also visited Joseph, confirming for him what was going on in his bride-to-be's life (Matthew 1:20–23). We do not know when Mary and Joseph talked through their angel stories, but after the visits from angels, Mary and Joseph lived together as husband and wife in Nazareth, although not having sexual relations until after Jesus was born (Matt. 1:24–25).

Luke placed the birth of Jesus in its historical setting. Caesar Augustus ruled from 30 B.C. to A.D. 14. He was the great-nephew of Julius Caesar. Quirinius was in charge of implementing a census or registration for taxation purposes, and secular records indicate he worked in some capacity in Syria in 6 B.C. Add Matthew's mention of Herod the Great, and the timing of Jesus' birth would have been before Herod died in 4 B.C. Some get confused about Jesus being born *before Christ* (B.C.). That problem arose with calendar makers centuries later, not with New Testament writers.

Both Matthew and Luke record events that support Jesus' birth as the fulfillment of prophecy. The Messiah was descended from David; Bethlehem was his home. Mary did not have to make the eighty-mile trip from Nazareth to Bethlehem, but she did, because Joseph was in the genealogical line from David to Joseph (Luke 3:20–37). Although Roman occupation and taxation were not popular in Israel, Joseph and Mary were like most—subdued and obedient, doing what they were told.

THE VIRGIN BIRTH

Mary said she was a virgin (Luke 1:34). An angel told Joseph that also (Matt. 1:23), which was backed up with a quotation from Isaiah 7:14. A Hebrew word in Isaiah 7:14 can be translated either *virgin* or *young woman*. The Greek Old Testament uses the word for *virgin*. Matthew 1:25 states that Mary and Joseph did not sexually consummate their marriage until after Jesus was born.

The virgin birth is not about some kind of god having sex with a helpless teenager. Rather, the virgin birth is about the God of this universe starting the birth process in a woman. Can God do that? My answer begins with the first five words of the Bible, "In the beginning, God created." Add to that the miracles and prophecies of the Bible. Consider the resurrection of Jesus. The miraculous conception and virgin birth are certainly within the capability of God, and add to our understanding of the birth of Jesus.

About 1,000 years after David, the descendants of David filled the small town of Bethlehem. Mary and Joseph could not find normal lodging. The innkeeper provided a place among the animals. In that setting, Jesus was born. Jesus was their firstborn, in a family that grew to at least four other sons and two daughters (Matt. 13:55).

The birth of Jesus is recorded simply: Mary "gave birth to her first born, a son. She wrapped him in cloths and placed him in a manger" (Luke 2:7). Later, that was a sign for the shepherds to find Jesus. Swaddling cloths were normal—a large strip of cloth with a longer strip coming from one corner. Jesus was first wrapped in the blanket, and then the long narrow strip was wrapped around him. The manger or feeding trough was the sign for the shepherds, for that is not where one normally looks for babies.

The last clause of Luke 2:7 is a reflection of what happened to Jesus at his birth as well as how he was later received in his ministry. Literally, no rooms were available, and that has no negative meaning for the innkeeper. These words, "there was no room for them in the inn" are often still true today in celebrations of Christmas as well as in our everyday lives. Everything about Jesus' birth sometimes gets celebrated except Jesus. We minimalize Jesus, crowd him out of our celebrations, and often have no room for him.

Listening to Angels (2:8–14)

She was only seven years old, but Ruth was enamored with the Christmas story, not about Santa Claus but about Jesus. She thought she heard something outside the window at the top of the stairwell. She sat there, looking intently at the snow. Her father, not a believer, but a caring father, said, "Ruth, Santa Claus can't come until you get to bed. He doesn't want to be seen doing his work." Ruth said, "Shhh, daddy, I am not looking for Santa; I'm listening for angels. I think I hear them. Will you listen with me?"

Listening to the angels is a good way to catch the meaning of the biblical accounts of Jesus' birth. Both Luke and Matthew feature several appearances of angels. The first ones to hear about the birth of Jesus were shepherds, caring for their sheep. Suddenly the night sky was filled with light. It was the "glory of the Lord." That phrase does not come with a definition, but God's radiance somehow lit up the sky. The shepherds were scared to death. Don't be too hard on them. Often when angels appeared, their first order of business was to say, "Do not be afraid" (Luke 2:10). If I were a shepherd or one of the other people, angels would have to deal with my fears also.

The angel's message is packed with profound meaning. Notice each component carefully.

- "Do not be afraid" (2:10).
- The angel brought "good news of great joy that will be for all the people" (2:10), not just a few or the elite.
- The birth took place in "the town of David" (2:11), as prophesied.
- Jesus is "Savior" (2:11).
- Jesus is "Christ" (2:11).
- Jesus is "the Lord" (2:11).

Luke 2:11 uses three titles to describe Jesus: "Savior," "Christ," and "Lord." Matthew also referred to Jesus in his Christmas story as "Christ" and "Immanuel" (Matt. 1:18, 23). One name cannot express enough. The word "Savior" shares a common meaning with the Hebrew word for Jesus, which means *God saves.* Jesus came to rescue and save us from our sins. As such, he is the Messiah (the Hebrew word) or Christ (the Greek term), each meaning the same. The promised and anointed one of God came to earth. "Lord" is the characteristic term of Matthew for the ruler and master. Some early Christians died because they refused to say *Caesar is Lord.* Jesus was their only Lord and Savior.

THE CHRISTMAS STORY IN MATTHEW

A second set of visitors, known as "the Magi," or *wise men*, visited Jesus later in Bethlehem (Matt. 2:1–11). They searched for Jesus. They presented gifts to Jesus and his family.

For what are you willing to search that demonstrates your devotion and discipleship? What are you willing to bring, not just of your finances but of all of your life, to lay at Jesus' feet? Consider how you can change so that you and others experience more deeply the One who is Savior, Christ, and Lord.

When the shepherds acted on the message, they had a sign that confirmed the baby's identity: a baby in a feeding trough. An inauspicious beginning for such a person.

Suddenly a host of angels joined the lone angel. What a heavenly choir! Essentially their praise moves in two directions: (1) "in the highest," praising and rejoicing in heaven and for all of heaven at Jesus' birth; and (2) "on earth," peace and good will. That reality of peace has not saturated the minds and hearts of people, churches, or nations, but that goal is still appropriate for all—peace with God, peace with one another.

Good News Is Too Good to Keep (2:15–20)

With God, all people are common and all are special, but God chose shepherds to be the first to hear about the birth. The image of a shepherd represents God in Psalm 23, and Jesus identified himself as the Good Shepherd (John 10:11). Shepherds have a rich tradition in the Bible, both through shepherds like Moses and David as well as in imagery related to God. However, the actual practice of shepherding in the first century had lost its aura. It was a dirty, stinking job, and if you could not do anything else, you became a shepherd. Interestingly, the Lord appeared first to them. They were first to hear the message of Jesus' birth, and then they became the first to tell it.

When the heavenly chorus departed, the shepherds said, "Let's go to Bethlehem" (Luke 2:15). So when the heavenly chorus departed, they "hurried off" to Bethlehem. They found Jesus and his parents. They saw. Their belief was confirmed, but the news was too good to keep to themselves. The first witnesses were first responders. They "spread the word." People were amazed. The shepherds went back to their jobs, praising God for what they had seen and heard. Luke adds, "just as they had been told" (2:20).

That's just the way God is. If God promises something, such as a Messiah in Bethlehem, he keeps his promise. When the time was right, he showed up. You can have a similar confidence in all of God's promises and instructions.

In the midst of the shepherds' praise, the Scripture paints a different picture of Mary. This teenage mother was surprised and astounded during the months of her pregnancy. Like most mothers, she probably had her moments of exhilaration, but now she "treasured up all these things and pondered them in her heart" (2:19). She wondered and thought. What an array of experiences Mary had. After Jesus' birth, she would be the means whereby Jesus relearned life as a baby growing toward adulthood. Mary treasured what had happened, but she kept some things to herself, pondering them. As time passed, we can be grateful that she probably shared them with a physician by the name of Luke, who wrote them down.

This Lesson and Life

When we began Upward basketball[1] at our church, my wife and I drove two third- and fourth-grade children to practices and games in early December. I asked them, "What's your favorite Christmas music?" Immediately, one said "Jingle Bells," and the other said, "Rudolf." One asked, "Bob, what's yours?" I said, "It's not just a Christmas song, but I like 'Jesus loves me.'" To that the boy asked, "Who is Jesus?" He got an answer that night, but my wife, our whole Upward program, and I knew that we had a blessed opportunity and privilege.

People are still around us who need to know about Jesus. You may be surprised at how little some know. People need to hear from folks just like us about the One who is Savior, Christ, and Lord. Likewise, many other people simply need someone to care about them and help them deal with life. Maybe you could be the extension of the peace and presence of God this Christmas. The God who used lowly shepherds many years ago can certainly use you today.

QUESTIONS

1. What fears do you have when it comes to being a disciple of Jesus Christ?

2. If you were a parent to Mary or Joseph, how would you handle the story of Mary's pregnancy?

3. How do you feel about people who work minimum-wage jobs or some less glamorous job that may leave them smelling worse than first-century shepherds?

4. How can you "spread the word" like the shepherds did?

5. What changes would you make in your life based on this statement: *If God promises it, I can do it?*

6. The word *angel* literally means *a messenger of God.* To whom can you be a messenger of God, and what can you do?

NOTES ——————————————————————————————

1. www.upward.org. Accessed 4/4/11.

Our Next New Study
(Available for use beginning March 2012)

AMOS, HOSEA, ISAIAH, MICAH:
Calling for Justice, Mercy, and Faithfulness

MICAH: GOD'S REQUIREMENTS

How to Order More Bible Study Materials

It's easy! Just fill in the following information. For additional Bible study materials available both in print and online, see www.baptistwaypress.org, or get a complete order form of available print materials—including Spanish materials—by calling 1-866-249-1799 or e-mailing baptistway@texasbaptists.org.

Title of item	Price	Quantity	Cost
This Issue:			
The Gospel of Matthew: A Primer for Discipleship—Study Guide (BWP001127)	$3.95	_____	_____
The Gospel of Matthew: A Primer for Discipleship—Large Print Study Guide (BWP001128)	$4.25	_____	_____
The Gospel of Matthew: A Primer for Discipleship—Teaching Guide (BWP001129)	$4.95	_____	_____
Additional Issues Available:			
Growing Together in Christ—Study Guide (BWP001036)	$3.25	_____	_____
Growing Together in Christ—Teaching Guide (BWP001038)	$3.75	_____	_____
Living Faith in Daily Life—Study Guide (BWP001095)	$3.55	_____	_____
Living Faith in Daily Life—Large Print Study Guide (BWP001096)	$3.95	_____	_____
Living Faith in Daily Life—Teaching Guide (BWP001097)	$4.25	_____	_____
Participating in God's Mission—Study Guide (BWP001077)	$3.55	_____	_____
Participating in God's Mission—Large Print Study Guide (BWP001078)	$3.95	_____	_____
Participating in God's Mission—Teaching Guide (BWP001079)	$3.95	_____	_____
Profiles in Character—Study Guide (BWP001112)	$3.55	_____	_____
Profiles in Character—Large Print Study Guide (BWP001113)	$4.25	_____	_____
Profiles in Character—Teaching Guide (BWP001114)	$4.95	_____	_____
Genesis: People Relating to God—Study Guide (BWP001088)	$2.35	_____	_____
Genesis: People Relating to God—Large Print Study Guide (BWP001089)	$2.75	_____	_____
Genesis: People Relating to God—Teaching Guide (BWP001090)	$2.95	_____	_____
Genesis 12—50: Family Matters—Study Guide (BWP000034)	$1.95	_____	_____
Genesis 12—50: Family Matters—Teaching Guide (BWP000035)	$2.45	_____	_____
Leviticus, Numbers, Deuteronomy—Study Guide (BWP000053)	$2.35	_____	_____
Leviticus, Numbers, Deuteronomy—Large Print Study Guide (BWP000052)	$2.35	_____	_____
Leviticus, Numbers, Deuteronomy—Teaching Guide (BWP000054)	$2.95	_____	_____
1 and 2 Samuel—Study Guide (BWP000002)	$2.35	_____	_____
1 and 2 Samuel—Large Print Study Guide (BWP000001)	$2.35	_____	_____
1 and 2 Samuel—Teaching Guide (BWP000003)	$2.95	_____	_____
1 and 2 Kings: Leaders and Followers—Study Guide (BWP001025)	$2.95	_____	_____
1 and 2 Kings: Leaders and Followers Large Print Study Guide (BWP001026)	$3.15	_____	_____
1 and 2 Kings: Leaders and Followers Teaching Guide (BWP001027)	$3.45	_____	_____
Ezra, Haggai, Zechariah, Nehemiah, Malachi—Study Guide (BWP001071)	$3.25	_____	_____
Ezra, Haggai, Zechariah, Nehemiah, Malachi—Large Print Study Guide (BWP001072)	$3.55	_____	_____
Ezra, Haggai, Zechariah, Nehemiah, Malachi—Teaching Guide (BWP001073)	$3.75	_____	_____
Job, Ecclesiastes, Habakkuk, Lamentations—Study Guide (BWP001016)	$2.75	_____	_____
Job, Ecclesiastes, Habakkuk, Lamentations—Large Print Study Guide (BWP001017)	$2.85	_____	_____
Job, Ecclesiastes, Habakkuk, Lamentations—Teaching Guide (BWP001018)	$3.25	_____	_____
Psalms and Proverbs—Study Guide (BWP001000)	$2.75	_____	_____
Psalms and Proverbs—Teaching Guide (BWP001002)	$3.25	_____	_____
Matthew: Hope in the Resurrected Christ—Study Guide (BWP001066)	$3.25	_____	_____
Matthew: Hope in the Resurrected Christ—Large Print Study Guide (BWP001067)	$3.55	_____	_____
Matthew: Hope in the Resurrected Christ—Teaching Guide (BWP001068)	$3.75	_____	_____
Mark: Jesus' Works and Words—Study Guide (BWP001022)	$2.95	_____	_____
Mark: Jesus' Works and Words—Large Print Study Guide (BWP001023)	$3.15	_____	_____
Mark:Jesus' Works and Words—Teaching Guide (BWP001024)	$3.45	_____	_____
Jesus in the Gospel of Mark—Study Guide (BWP000066)	$1.95	_____	_____
Jesus in the Gospel of Mark—Teaching Guide (BWP000067)	$2.45	_____	_____
Luke: Journeying to the Cross—Study Guide (BWP000057)	$2.35	_____	_____
Luke: Journeying to the Cross—Large Print Study Guide (BWP000056)	$2.35	_____	_____
Luke: Journeying to the Cross—Teaching Guide (BWP000058)	$2.95	_____	_____
The Gospel of John: Light Overcoming Darkness, Part One—Study Guide (BWP001104)	$3.55	_____	_____
The Gospel of John: Light Overcoming Darkness, Part One—Large Print Study Guide (BWP001105)	$3.95	_____	_____
The Gospel of John: Light Overcoming Darkness, Part One—Teaching Guide (BWP001106)	$4.50	_____	_____
The Gospel of John: Light Overcoming Darkness, Part Two—Study Guide (BWP001109)	$3.55	_____	_____
The Gospel of John: Light Overcoming Darkness, Part Two—Large Print Study Guide (BWP001110)	$3.95	_____	_____
The Gospel of John: Light Overcoming Darkness, Part Two—Teaching Guide (BWP001111)	$4.50	_____	_____
The Gospel of John: The Word Became Flesh—Study Guide (BWP001008)	$2.75	_____	_____
The Gospel of John: The Word Became Flesh—Large Print Study Guide (BWP001009)	$2.85	_____	_____
The Gospel of John: The Word Became Flesh—Teaching Guide (BWP001010)	$3.25	_____	_____
Acts: Toward Being a Missional Church—Study Guide (BWP001013)	$2.75	_____	_____
Acts: Toward Being a Missional Church—Large Print Study Guide (BWP001014)	$2.85	_____	_____
Acts: Toward Being a Missional Church—Teaching Guide (BWP001015)	$3.25	_____	_____
Romans: What God Is Up To—Study Guide (BWP001019)	$2.95	_____	_____
Romans: What God Is Up To—Large Print Study Guide (BWP001020)	$3.15	_____	_____
Romans: What God Is Up To—Teaching Guide (BWP001021)	$3.45	_____	_____

The Corinthian Letters—Study Guide (BWP001121)	$3.55	_____	_____
The Corinthian Letters—Large Print Study Guide (BWP001122)	$4.25	_____	_____
The Corinthian Letters—Teaching Guide (BWP001123)	$4.95	_____	_____
Galatians and 1&2 Thessalonians—Study Guide (BWP001080)	$3.55	_____	_____
Galatians and 1&2 Thessalonians—Large Print Study Guide (BWP001081)	$3.95	_____	_____
Galatians and 1&2 Thessalonians—Teaching Guide (BWP001082)	$3.95	_____	_____
Ephesians, Philippians, Colossians—Study Guide (BWP001060)	$3.25	_____	_____
Ephesians, Philippians, Colossians—Teaching Guide (BWP001062)	$3.75	_____	_____
1, 2 Timothy, Titus, Philemon—Study Guide (BWP000092)	$2.75	_____	_____
1, 2 Timothy, Titus, Philemon—Teaching Guide (BWP000093)	$3.25	_____	_____
Letters of James and John—Study Guide (BWP001101)	$3.55	_____	_____
Letters of James and John—Large Print Study Guide (BWP001102)	$3.95	_____	_____
Letters of James and John—Teaching Guide (BWP001103)	$4.25	_____	_____
Revelation—Study Guide (BWP000084)	$2.35	_____	_____
Revelation—Large Print Study Guide (BWP000083)	$2.35	_____	_____

Coming for use beginning March 2012

Amos. Hosea, Isaiah, Micah: Calling for Justice, Mercy, and Faithfulness—Study Guide (BWP001132)	$3.95	_____	_____
Amos. Hosea, Isaiah, Micah: Calling for Justice, Mercy, and Faithfulness—Large Print Study Guide (BWP001133)	$4.25	_____	_____
Amos. Hosea, Isaiah, Micah: Calling for Justice, Mercy, and Faithfulness—Teaching Guide (BWP001134)	$4.95	_____	_____

Cost
of items (Order value)   _____

Shipping charges
(see chart*)   _____

TOTAL   _____

Standard (UPS/Mail) Shipping Charges*			
Order Value	Shipping charge**	Order Value	Shipping charge**
$.01—$9.99	$6.50	$160.00—$199.99	$24.00
$10.00—$19.99	$8.50	$200.00—$249.99	$28.00
$20.00—$39.99	$9.50	$250.00—$299.99	$30.00
$40.00—$59.99	$10.50	$300.00—$349.99	$34.00
$60.00—$79.99	$11.50	$350.00—$399.99	$42.00
$80.00—$99.99	$12.50	$400.00—$499.99	$50.00
$100.00—$129.99	$15.00	$500.00—$599.99	$60.00
$130.00—$159.99	$20.00	$600.00—$799.99	$72.00**

*Plus, applicable taxes for individuals and other taxable entities (not churches) within Texas will be added. Please call 1-866-249-1799 if the exact amount is needed prior to ordering.

**For order values $800.00 and above, please call 1-866-249-1799 or check www.baptistwaypress.org

Please allow three weeks for standard delivery. For express shipping service: Call 1-866-249-1799 for information on additional charges.

YOUR NAME _____   PHONE _____

YOUR CHURCH _____   DATE ORDERED _____

SHIPPING ADDRESS _____

CITY _____   STATE _____   ZIP CODE _____

E-MAIL _____

MAIL this form with your check for the total amount to
BAPTISTWAY PRESS, Baptist General Convention of Texas,
333 North Washington, Dallas, TX 75246-1798
(Make checks to "Baptist Executive Board.")

OR, **FAX** your order anytime to: 214-828-5376, and we will bill you.

OR, **CALL** your order toll-free: 1-866-249-1799
(M-Fri 8:30 a.m.-5:00 p.m. central time), and we will bill you.

OR, **E-MAIL** your order to our internet e-mail address:
baptistway@texasbaptists.org, and we will bill you.

OR, **ORDER ONLINE** at www.baptistwaypress.org.

We look forward to receiving your order! Thank you!